The M
Gave Away
His Lottery Win

A conversation with a remarkable man
about the way we communicate

Phillip Khan-Panni

PKP Communicators

The man who gave away his Lottery win

By Phillip Khan-Panni

© Copyright 2019

The right of Phillip Khan-Panni to be identified as the author of this work is asserted in accordance with sections 77 and 78 of the Copyright, Designs and Patents Act of 1988.

All rights reserved. No part of this publication may be reproduced in any material form *(including photocopying or storing in any medium by electronic means and whether or not transiently or incidentally to some other use of this publication) without the written permission of the copyright holder except in accordance with the provisions of the Copyright, Designs and Patents Act 1988. Applications for the copyright holder's written permission to reproduce any part of this publication should be addressed directly to the author.*

ISBN: 9781796519143

Other books by the author:

- 2-4-6-8, How do you communicate?
- Blank page to first draft in 15 minutes
- Stand & Deliver: leave them stirred not shaken
- Be the best Best Man & make a stunning speech (re-issued as) How to make a brilliant Best Man's speech
- Getting your point across
- (The FT Guide to) Making Business Presentations
- Rhyme & Reason: my life in rhyme & poems for all occasions
- Wild Daisies (partial memoir)

Co-author of:
- Communicating across cultures
- Make more sales with better presentations

For EVELYN
Endlessly supportive

CONTENTS

Preface   **9**

Chapter 1: Blackfriars incident   **11**

Among the hurrying London commuters, I see a grey-haired man give a homeless person a watch and £50. The man was stunned by the caring of a complete stranger. It prompts an idea for my next speech at Toastmasters: about a man who made a difference to someone's day, and why he chose to give a watch.

Chapter 2: Once again   **19**

One month later, the scene is repeated at Victoria: watches & £50 to two rough sleepers. I meet the grey-haired man, Norman Sinclair, a retired copywriter. A big lottery win set him free to pursue a private project. I was to learn his ideas about the true meaning of communication. We agree to meet at his home next day.

Chapter 3: About the Lottery win   **29**

I visit Norman in Surrey. Norman explains what he did with his big lottery win, and why. His purpose is to improve relationships, on a personal level and also more widely. He likes the direct contact with the homeless individuals he helps. However, his focus is on connecting the mind of the speaker with that of the listener.

Chapter 4: First Truth about communication   **39**

We talked about the essence of good communication. Was it having a simple message, expressed clearly? Norman explained his theory of verbal communication, mentioning Hamilton's Postulate and the Language of Thought Hypothesis that focuses on the attitude behind what we say.

Chapter 5: Second Truth about communication 49

Instead of speaking to be understood, we should speak to avoid being misunderstood. Some historical catastrophes resulted from miscommunication. What was intended and what was heard were different, largely because of what the listener in each case expected to hear.

Chapter 6: Third truth of communication 57

Successful communication depends on how you make your listeners feel. The language you use can override your intention, so always think about the likely effect of the words you use. People buy on emotion and justify with reason, so you should first aim to make your listeners or prospects feel good. That's what Robert Cialdini calls Pre-suasion.

Chapter 7: Five questions 65

Understand that people develop habits and their buying decisions follow an ecosystem. That explains why a product that is superior to the market leader may never overtake it. I mention Better Mousetrap thinking and why The Nook will always lag behind Kindle. The speakers' dilemma is whether to speak about their expertise or their Added Value.

Chapter 8: Getting acceptance 75

Is the target audience business or lay? It's people. However, always concentrate on those who have a need for what you are offering. We construct an imaginary scene of an 18th century courtier delivering a vital message to the king, to highlight five essential elements of communication.

Chapter 9: Does your wife snore? 87

Norman tells the story of Copywriter Bill who had a problem with accepting criticism of his work by those he considered his intellectual inferiors. Bill's thinking was adjusted by being asked an unexpected question. When we give feedback, it is important not to sound prescriptive, and that's where the Tag Question comes in.

Chapter 10: Lunch break   99

Norman prepares a vegan meal, explaining why he had turned off meat and started eating only 'living food'. He says he now takes time to smell the roses. King Henry VIII and Napoleon carried illnesses that affected their behaviour and possibly their judgement too. Norman drew the distinction between the Sick Role and the Impaired Role.

Chapter 11: Taking it personally   107

We talked about haggling in an Eastern market, and how westerners often fail to understand how the shopkeeper engages with the customer and creates an obligation to buy. An essential part of the transaction is always to allow the other to save face. Norman mentioned Schopenhauer's example of how porcupines keep warm together, offering four rules for safeguarding a relationship.

Chapter 12: What's the story?   119

Norman told me about a professional speaker who tells other speakers to tell stories in their speeches. Present them as mini stage plays full of dialogue, to bring the story to life and enable your listeners to re-create your message by remembering the story. I told him my own story of Charlie, the awkward fat boy from whose example I learned a valuable lesson. Norman talked about neural coupling.

Chapter 13: Meeting expectations   131

A story will keep your listeners engaged. It's part of the effect you have on them. But be careful of how your listeners feel when you replace their long-held beliefs with your own ideas. We are talking about understanding the process of communication, about creating and managing the expectations of the audience. There are four such expectations.

Chapter 14: Listening   141

The most underrated skill in verbal communication is listening. There is a difference between telling to inform and telling to educate. So always verify what your audience has taken in. We all have embedded assumptions which make us hear what we expect rather than what was actually said. And why we can use language that tricks the listener into hearing what we did not say.

Chapter 15: Miscommunication   153

There are several ways in which we mislead others. We might make an incorrect claim or statement, or deliberately use the wrong word to see what reaction we would get. Who would have the nerve to correct us? Politicians, among others, are practised in deception by implication or by omission. Why should we care about such things? Because we must talk to one another more, avoiding manipulations.

Chapter 16: The language we use   163

Persuasion in language recognises the roles of Dominant and Supplicant. The Dominant has the power while the Supplicant has the need. The roles will determine the language we use. The Milton Model, used in NLP and hypnosis, embeds instructions and commands in indirect suggestions, engaging the listener's mind so that the necessary action takes place.

Chapter 17: Closure   173

A trying phone call with someone in Customer Services at my electricity supplier. My quest for advice was translated into a complaint, just to enable a box to be ticked. Reminded myself of the Three Truths of Communication and my own Five Questions when outlining my business presentation. Dropping in on Norman the next day, I encountered an unexpected finale. Or was it a new beginning?

About the author   185

8

Preface

The idea for the title of this book came from something I did myself. I wondered how such an unusual gesture would actually be received.

It provided me with the framework for my reflections on the way we communicate with one another. I thought a conversation between two people would be easy to read and take in. There has been a rash of stage shows in which actors conduct conversations with themselves and with the audience. So I was comfortable with the format.

The characters are, of course, fictitious – composites of people I have known. A few are actual people, whose wisdom I quoted and wanted to acknowledge. However, although written as a novel, this is not really a work of fiction. You may find yourself nodding and declaring, "That's just what I would say!" I hope you do.

This is not intended to be a how-to book, but one that might prompt you to pause and reflect on the way you connect with others around you. You are invited to eavesdrop on the extended chat between two like-minded people and decide if you like what they say.

If you do, please tell others.

Phillip Khan-Panni
Ireland, 2019

THE MAN WHO GAVE AWAY HIS LOTTERY WIN

One

Blackfriars incident

On an overcast morning in September I saw something that would lead to an amazing encounter. I was in the surge of passengers exiting the trains at London's Blackfriars station, on my way to a meeting at the London Chamber for Commerce and Industry. There is an urgency in commuter crowds, a burst of rapidly-striding people spilling out on to the street, then quickly thinning out as they choose the channels to their final destinations. It's like an explosion of energy that shoves you in the small of your back, then suddenly abandons you, leaving you to make your own next move, as you pause in the early morning mist.

In that billowing wave of people, you can notice someone marching to the beat of a different drum, and on that morning that's what caught my eye. On the pavement outside the station was a rough sleeper huddled in his dark and tatty sleeping bag, close by a drain pipe that trickled water past him. His was sitting up, at his feet a cardboard coffee cup acting as a begging

11

bowl, within his reach but sufficiently distant to allow passers-by to drop in some money without having to engage with him or catch his eye. The commuters all hurried by, focused on their journey to work, treating him like street furniture, a commonplace sight that was too familiar to attract attention or compassion. All except one man.

Grey haired and well-dressed in a dark suit, he stopped beside the Homeless Man and asked the time. The man was taken by surprise and said, "Huh?" Grey Hair repeated the question, tapping his own right wrist for emphasis. Homeless Man was scruffy and unshaven, and clearly had no reason to rise and greet the day, or even to engage in conversation with a passing stranger. In reply he pointed at his own empty wrist, shook his head and said, "I don't have a watch."

"WHAT TIME IS IT?"

At this Grey Hair pulled a watch from his pocket, checked the time it was showing against the wristwatch on his own left wrist, and handed the "spare" to Homeless Man. "Now you do have a watch," he said, gently, as he drew a £50 note from his pocket and handed that over as well, saying, "Thought you might need this too." The sleeper's mouth opened wide and he seemed too shocked to say anything. He started to rise in an instinctive gesture of respect for the only act of kindness he had received in a long time. But Grey Hair placed a hand on his shoulder to stop him rising, smiled at him, then walked quickly away, not waiting for any thanks. Job done.

The transaction took less than 15 seconds, and I noticed it mainly because it had a different rhythm from the milling multitudes, and I watched Grey Hair striding away, disappearing down the steps into the pedestrian underpass. I went on my own way, but the incident stayed with me all day, and into the evening when I sat at my desk at home to prepare a speech for the next Toastmasters meeting in Bromley.

Why had I noticed the incident, I asked myself. After all, it was not uncommon for someone to give money to a homeless person. Perhaps it was the watch, and the amount of money, rather more than the usual handout. Then it struck me: it had seemed like a practised incident, as though Grey Hair had done it before and was well prepared. What was behind it, I had wondered. But I'd been on my way to a business meeting and had things on my mind, so I'd let the incident pass. Just another interesting episode in London life.

I remembered it as I sat to prepare the speech I had to deliver at Toastmasters. It was The Motivational Speech from the Advanced Manual, The Professional Speaker. Its purpose was to inspire the audience to take some action, applying a structured approach. The Blackfriars incident would fit well into the speech. As a professional speaker, I already had a couple of well-prepared speeches, but I did not want to deliver those at Toastmasters. I wanted to try out some new material.

THE PURPOSE OF MOTIVATION?

What was the incident's relevance to my speech? The Manual says, "What is the purpose of motivation? It is to cause others to think, believe, and act as you want them to ... and have them like it." I winced a little at the Americanism at the end of that sentence, but I got the point. Your listeners must want to make the change. The Manual goes on to state that there is a 3-step process to achieve that objective:

- State your proposal clearly
- Eliminate any conflicting ideas
- Show the advantages of the proposal

I was surprised that the Manual did not add the 4th step – the call to action. There's little point in arousing enthusiasm for some new point of view if you don't tell people what to do about it. Reading the Manual more closely, I noticed that it had been badly edited. The call to action was there, but on the next page, and the four-part process recommended was:

- Get attention
- Create vivid pictures in the listeners' minds
- Dramatise the speech, acting out the relevant passages
- Call to action

14

It still didn't feel right. It's not that I disagreed with any of that, but it felt like something was missing. Perhaps it was because I was remembering the Blackfriars incident and wondering how to fit it in. As a matter of fact, there seemed to be a conflict between the incident and the structure of the speech recommended by the Manual. The latter seemed to have been written by someone who knew the mechanics of speech making but had no feeling for the process of persuasion or motivation.

What was it about Grey Hair that was getting in the way of this speech? I had to step away from my desk and give it some thought. Here was a man who obviously set out to make a difference to someone else's day. He'd thought about it, decided who would be the person he could help, and prepared his gift. I tried to put myself in his shoes and think like him. What would a homeless person need? Shelter, food and money, obviously. In the short term, he could not provide shelter. He could provide food, but that would entail engaging with the person, and it might even cause some embarrassment. Money would allow the person to make his own choice about food.

And what else? What else could one provide? The more I thought about it, the more I related to the dynamics of the Blackfriars incident. A rough sleeper would be unlikely to have any valuable possessions left. A watch would have been pawned or sold long ago, but a watch represents a connection with the world that had cast him adrift. You need a watch to tell you when to connect with events around you. It was such a significant gift! And anything else?

STUNNED BY THE CARING

The choice of a watch as a gift told me about Grey Hair's thinking – his empathy. But I remembered the look on the face of Homeless Man. He was stunned by the caring. In his situation, it must have been a long time since anyone showed him any caring, and that's why he found it so difficult to respond immediately. He had tried to rise in a show of respect, but the words wouldn't come.

Now I understood. I grasped the meaning of all that had happened in those highly-charged 15 seconds on the pavement outside Blackfriars station on an otherwise dull September morning. It's amazing how much can happen in such a short span of time, and how much one can learn from it, just by taking the time to think about it.

What, then, would be the message of my speech?

I think it was that final realisation that mattered most: the effect on the person to whom we show some caring. That's when I started thinking about gift giving. Soon it would be time to consider Christmas and the gifts we would exchange. The socks that no one wanted, the boxes of chocolates that were the easy option, the gizmos that might amuse but never get used, all chosen, wrapped and delivered without an ounce of caring, all just providing evidence that we had done our duty.

What change did I want to bring about? I could do a speech on the giving of gifts, on the thought that we should put into the choice, on the effect it might have on the recipient, and most of all, how the gift might make a difference to the relationship. It would no longer be a speech that mechanically followed a recommended structure, It would be about something I strongly believed in. And I had a story to tell, to illustrate how powerful it could be to think carefully about the right gift.

Little did I know what I would learn from that incident.

Chapter 1 Summary

Blackfriars Incident

Among the hurrying London commuters, I see a grey-haired man give a homeless person a watch and £50. The man was stunned by the caring of a complete stranger.

It prompts an idea for a speech at Toastmasters, from the Motivational Manual for experienced speakers. The sequence I decided to follow was:
- Get attention
- Paint vivid word pictures
- Use drama
- Call to action

Thoughts that stay with me, about the incident:
- A man who decided to make a difference to someone's day
- Why a watch? To connect the person with the world around him
- What does that say about the giver? Empathy
- Think carefully about the gift you choose: focus on the receiver

THE MAN WHO GAVE AWAY HIS LOTTERY WIN

Two

Once again

A month later, at the start of a sunny day, when it was bright but not yet warm, I went up to London to shop at the House of Fraser in Victoria Street. Strolling along the covered section of Victoria Street, past the paper seller and the fruit and veg stall, I noticed a rough sleeper propped up against one of the shop windows, benefitting from the warm air being blown from a vent in the pavement. He had a begging cup beside him and a hand-written sign stating, "HOMELESS, PLEASE HELP".

It reminded me instantly of the Blackfriars incident. Suddenly I noticed a man in a light grey overcoat with a black velvet collar stop by the beggar to ask the time. It was a repeat of the Blackfriars incident of a month before, and something went ping! inside my head. I stopped and pretended to look in the shop window, just so I could observe the giving of a watch and a £50 note.

The benefactor, whom I recognised as Grey Hair from last month, quickly moved on, and I followed. He was slim, of medium height and fit looking. Perhaps in his late 50s, possibly 60, as I had thought when I first saw him at Blackfriars. He walked on unhurriedly, but with purpose in his stride. 30 yards further down the street was another rough sleeper, this time in a reddish sleeping bag. He had no sign to declare his plight, but he was obviously homeless. His fair hair was dirty and matted, his face was smudged, he looked about 20 years old, and very unhappy.

I HAD TO FIND OUT

I kept my distance as Grey Hair approached the second Homeless Man and repeated the business with a watch and a £50 note. Once again, there was the incredulous reaction, the declined gratitude and the swift walking away. It was the most amazing thing. I had to find out what it was all about, so I lengthened my stride and caught up with Grey Hair.

"That was the most astonishing thing I have seen for many a year," I said, as I drew alongside. "Do you mind if I ask you why you are doing it?"

He stopped and turned to face me, with a beaming smile. "I think he was pleased, don't you?" he said. I was taken aback, having expected no more than a polite thanks. Clearly he was willing to talk about it.

"And so was the other chap back there, and also the fellow at Blackfriars, last month," I replied.

"Oh, were you there then?" he asked, looking puzzled by the coincidence.

"Yes I was," I replied, "by sheer chance. Thought I recognised you. They couldn't believe it, and neither could I. Tell me, why did you do it?"

"For the two best reasons in the world: because I could and because I wanted to."

"I could understand the money, but why the watch?"

"Oh, that's incidental," he shrugged, "It's just that I have acquired a number of watches that I'll never use, so I might as well give them away to those who need them. Perhaps it was a bit more than that. I thought to myself, what does a homeless person need, apart from shelter, food and money? It struck me that they almost certainly would not have a watch. So why not give them one? There's nothing quite like the pleasure you get from owning something really useful. Of course, I should have remembered to give them smaller denomination notes. Might be hard for them to buy a snack with a fifty. Someone might think they had nicked it."

A REMARKABLE MAN

As we spoke we quite naturally started walking again and I said, "You seem to be a remarkable man. I wish I knew what lay behind those acts of kindness. Judging from the reactions I saw, it was your kindness, your caring, that seemed to matter more than the watch and the money."

"Yes, I suppose you are right," he said, "and I'll be glad to tell you the story, if you have the time."

"I have the time, and I have the inclination too," I declared. "Let me buy you a coffee," as we were right outside a coffee bar. We went inside and he told me one of the most incredible stories I think I have ever heard. We sat at a little table just inside the door, and our coffees were brought to us. It was time we introduced ourselves.

"My name is Norman Sinclair," he said, holding out his right hand, adding, "I'm a retired copywriter, a wordsmith, if you like. What about you, what do you do?"

I said I was also a wordsmith, a professional speaker and trainer in communication skills; I'd been a Sales Manager before that. His eyes lit up. "How brilliant! You're exactly the man I wanted to meet!" I looked puzzled, and he continued, "You see, I've been working on an idea that I want to share with professional speakers, for them to build into their speeches. It's all connected to why I've been giving away money and things."

Norman Sinclair was Scottish but he had lived in and around London most of his working life. His wife had died of cancer nearly twenty years ago. The trauma had caused him to quit his job and go freelance, giving himself the space and time to grieve without the obligations of a full-time job. He had done well and earned enough for a comfortable life.

"And then, about five years ago," he added, lowering his voice, "I had a big win on the Lottery. Multiple millions. I stopped working, sold up and bought myself a little bungalow in a quiet spot near the Kent and Surrey border."

"So that's when you retired?"

"In a sense, yes, that's when I stopped working for money. But I didn't stop working. I started two projects, which I'll tell you about in a moment, but first I want you to tell me about yourself, and what you do."

THE RIGHT CONDUIT

Now the boot was on the other foot and I had to explain who I was, what I spoke about, professionally, and explain the precarious world of a professional speaker. He explained that he needed to know that I was the right "conduit" for his story, if that's what I was going to be. He said he had spent the past five years sorting himself out and deciding what he wanted to do with the rest of his life.

I told him I used to work in national newspapers, first in advertising sales and then in editorial. I wrote pieces for one of the Diaries, and an occasional article on consumer affairs. That developed a sense of what it takes to get a story published in newspapers, and I began to help companies write their press releases. From there it was a small jump to providing training in presentation skills and public relations (PR), leaving full time employment to set up my own consultancy.

Soon I was being invited to speak at conferences on media, on public speaking and PR, and had to decide on a fee structure. Having never started out to be a professional speaker, I had no idea what to charge or how to structure a platform speech. Help came when I was approached by an event organiser from Singapore who said, "I like what you say about media and the way you speak from the platform, but would you mind if I gave you some guidance? It will help you get more work of that kind."

Naturally I accepted his offer of help with alacrity. He was rather direct (Singaporeans can be quite plain-spoken) and I had no reservations about taking advice. He sent me links to some video clips on YouTube, and also to a couple of Keynote speakers, telling me to copy them. By studying the videos he suggested, I got to know how to structure my talk. I got to understand what was expected of speakers. I also started practising my speeches more than ever before, and noticed how much better I looked and sounded on the platform.

Inevitably, my bookings were far from regular, and based entirely on recommendations and word of mouth. I needed to do some proper marketing. Sinclair stopped me then and said, "I'd like to know more about that, but not now, not today. I just want to tell you a couple of things before we go."

That gave me a pang of disappointment. I had not yet learned what was the story behind this man's unusual generosity to strangers, but we were coming to the end of an extraordinary encounter. There was so much more I wanted to know.

"I told you at the start that I had embarked on two projects when I retired to my bungalow outside London. Would you like to know what they were?"

I perked up. "Yes please!"

TWO NEW PROJECTS

"One was to change the way I lived my life, the other was to reflect on the way we communicate with each other. In a way, they are both connected to each other. Man is a social animal and communication, verbal communication in particular, is the essential exchange of the life force. I set about making myself as healthy as possible, and reflecting on how we should communicate with each other. The better your state of being, the more effectively you will communicate. Does that make sense?" I nodded.

"Let me offer you some evidence. How old do you think I am?"

I recalled my first impression of a man nudging 60, when I saw him with the first Homeless Man. So that was my answer. He just smiled, then said, "Actually I'm 79. I'll be 80 in a few months' time."

It would be a massive understatement to say I was stunned! Norman Sinclair was clearly not a young man, but his face was unlined, his skin was clear and his eyes sparkled with energy. What was his secret? I really wanted to know. But before I could ask, he touched me on the arm and said, "I know, you find it hard to believe, and you are probably wondering what's my secret. Well, I'll tell you about my life-changing routine, but that's for the next time we meet.

"First let me quickly tell you about my other project. I have spent the past five years thinking about the way we communicate with each other. As a wordsmith, verbal communication was my stock in trade. My copywriting was all about persuasion, using the power of words to induce people to do or buy certain things. But I realised that most active communication – and persuasion especially – is a one-way street. It involves my saying or doing something to influence you. But communication, true communication, is a two-way street.

"My mission is to enlighten people about a better way to get their point across without confusion, and to improve inter-personal connections. Tell me, would those skills be important to you?" He looked me straight in the eye. I could not break the eye contact, so I just nodded my head slowly as I thought about it. "Yes," I said finally, "I would want to be able to do those things."

THE INVITATION

"I'll tell you everything the next time we meet. When can you come down to my house?"

Suddenly the unexpected encounter with this remarkable man was about to end, and there was so much more I wanted to know about him. I knew I had things to do the next day, but I could easily put them off till another day.

"I could clear my diary and come down tomorrow, if that suits you," I offered. "But tell me, what are we going to talk about?"

"We'll explore the true meaning of communication, we'll talk about what goes on in our minds when we have something to say, and what happens when we are receiving the ideas of someone else. Most of all, we'll consider how effectively we get our point across, in business and in private conversations, and what can be done to improve that."

"I'll be up for that," I replied.

"Good," he said, reaching into the breast pocket of his jacket. "Here's my card. Come tomorrow. Aim to get to me about 10:30 in the morning, and we'll talk. There's much to say. Bring a notebook and a pen, that's all. I'll make us a spot of lunch, Vegetarian. Is that OK with you?"

"Oh yes, "I said. "I'll see you tomorrow." We shook hands and parted in Victoria Street, as he headed for the station and I continued my trip to the Army & Navy, my head buzzing with all I'd heard. I could hardly wait until the next instalment.

Chapter 2 Summary

ONCE AGAIN

One month later, the scene is repeated at Victoria: watches & £50 to two rough sleepers

I meet the grey-haired man, Norman Sinclair.

Norman Sinclair: retired copywriter
- Older than he looks
- Scottish but lived in London most of his life
- Wife died of cancer nearly 20 years ago
- Big lottery win set him free to pursue private project

Me: professional speaker, trainer in communication skills
- Former Sales Manager
- Worked in national newspapers: ad sales then editorial
- Helped companies with press releases
- Set up own consultancy to train in presentation skills & PR

I was to learn his ideas about the true meaning of communication.

We agree to meet at Norman Sinclair's Surrey bungalow next day

THE MAN WHO GAVE AWAY HIS LOTTERY WIN

Three

About the Lottery win

The following day I drove down to Norman Sinclair's house at Crockham Hill, not far from Westerham. Set back from the road, it was on a rise and shielded on three sides by tall trees that were sufficiently far away to cast their shadows away from the house. He had chosen well, if it was seclusion he wanted. The garden was neat with flower-filled borders and a billiard table lawn. Norman's Mercedes was in the open garage.

He greeted me warmly and led me to the conservatory at the back of the house, and seated me on a comfortable sofa, while he made us both mugs of tea, then sat directly in front of me so that were face to face. There was a comfortable warmth throughout, and the bungalow was remarkably spacious, with light oak furniture and bright lights. But no leather. He was, after all, vegetarian. Noticing me looking around, he explained, "I like brightness, so I avoided brown furniture. If I favour any style in the décor, it's probably a bit Scandinavian. No need for cosiness, as I live alone."

"Tell me about your lottery win," I asked as I sipped my tea. "What did you do with it? And why did you give it away?"

"Well, for one thing, I'd never spend it all. I won't live long enough, and anyway I already have everything I need. When I won the money, I booked myself into a posh hotel, just to feel rich, but also because I wanted to take time away from home while I decided what to do with the rest of my life. I don't know if you'll understand this, but I did not want any of that to change the way I felt about my home, my nest, this place. I did not want to stand here, in this room, feeling it was inadequate in any way, and that I now had the chance to improve on it.

"Over the previous two years I'd had 50 small wins on the lottery. Fifty. And then the big jackpot. It was almost as though the small wins were preparing me for the big one. Now at last I could do whatever I wanted, so I did a couple of sensible things right away. I gave my two children enough money to make them financially independent, and I arranged to have enough income for a comfortable life myself. The rest I decided to give away.

GAVE AWAY THE MONEY

"Who got the money?" I suppose we all have a theoretical list of people we'd include in a big lottery win, and it was natural to speculate on what anyone would do, in his position.

"Well, you learn a lot about people when you have a lot of money to give away. And about yourself as well!

My first thought was to help with some natural disaster in the third world, like earthquakes, floods or famine. No good trying to donate directly. All kinds of restrictions on foreign money going into those countries. You have to go through established charities, and they are not all the same. There is a body that rates them out of 4, so always look for a charity with a rating of 3 or 4.

"Then you have to check their actual performance. For example, following the Nepal earthquake of 2015, someone called Maxim Shrestha wrote that there was the largest international humanitarian Assistance and Disaster Response Mission for India and China, but many who went to the aid of Nepal didn't understand or anticipate the challenges of the topography. Villages in high mountains are not very accessible. As a result, vital aid was delayed in arriving.

"There was a cultural misunderstanding as well. To some in the Far East, such as the displaced middle class persons, second-hand clothing is not acceptable, unless you are totally destitute, and blankets were not needed in the Nepalese summer. So there was a lot of wasted generosity, and although I contributed to that relief fund, I did not throw all my money at it. But, you know, if you want to make a difference to large scale projects, such as homelessness, you need very deep pockets. Only governments have that sort of money. I had to think of something else. There was another reason too."

Pausing for a moment to collect his thoughts, Norman then went on to explain that he had no desire for publicity. If it became known that he was giving millions to any particular cause, it would have made headlines. It would have brought him attention that he did not want. It might even have resulted in his being offered an honour, which he also did not want. He explained all that diffidently, not wanting to sound egotistical. That was also why he did not want to endow a trust and perpetuate his name. But a little at a time, supporting carefully selected causes, he gave away much, but not all, of his surplus cash. He said he always felt cautious about giving it all away, "because then you have no more power to influence change."

THEME CONNECTING CAUSES?

"Is there a common theme connecting your chosen causes?" I asked, and he smiled.

"Yes, of course there is. Most of my donations have been to activities and organisations that further the cause of improving communication in business and between nations. It seems to me that many of the world's problems are either caused or exacerbated by faulty communication. There is now a vital need to correct that. Why now more than before? Because technology has enabled worldwide instant communication, and that has created more problems than ever before. Problems of bad communication.

"The US President speaks directly to millions through his tweets, but what does he say? And what lies behind that practice? He's a rabble rouser, bypassing the established channels of government. And what he says is often described as childish, petulant and inflammatory. There are, as well, many examples of bullying through social media. The channels of communication are increasingly in the hands of a small number of people who have neither the commitment nor the means to monitor and modify that communication. I mean the Facebooks and Twitters of this world. It is in their own interests to allow controversy. Because that generates more reader traffic, more involvement, and more pairs of eyes for advertisers. That's how they make their money.

"So what's the answer? It starts with education. Not just in schools and colleges, but in places of work and in every place where people look for knowledge and guidance. What do I mean by education? I mean changing the way people think and behave. It rests with those who have influence over the values and attitudes that govern our interpersonal behaviour. I put multiple millions into a Trust with a brief to provide courses in communication skills. I may put you in touch with them. That way the money will continue to provide the means to improve the way people communicate and avoid being misunderstood. I have people developing new programmes now. They will be turned into online courses which will generate new money and keep the process going. You could become a part of that process. You and others like you.

"When you speak in public, and when you write your books, you have it in your power to bring about change in the thinking, attitude and behaviour of those who listen to you. I'd like to encourage you to become conscious of the nature of your message. Instead of just telling people about your specialist subject, instead of just sharing your knowledge and your ideas, perhaps you should … but let me take a small step back and explain my main purpose.

"It is simply to improve relationships. Bad communication is possibly the most common cause of relationships breaking down, and most of the problems in the world. That applies in personal relationships but also in national and international issues. You can see how dangerous it is when the leaders of two nuclear powers started threatening each other with their nuclear buttons – *Mine is bigger than yours!*" and so on.

"Brexit is another example. Putting aside the final outcome, just remember how it split the nation. Opinions replaced facts, wishful thinking and special interests took precedence over common sense and informed analysis. Families and friends found themselves at odds as never before. And why? Because of bad communication. But I'll return to that later."

He broke off and held up a hand to stop himself, adding, "But I'm getting ahead of myself. I'll explain what I have in mind in a little while, when I run through my simple ideas for more effective communication. My focus is on helping people to understand the process of communication, i.e. what happens when people speak to each other. I'll come back to that as well in a little while."

That sounded intriguing, but I held back from asking any questions about it. He would tell me in his own time, but I was becoming increasingly fascinated by this man and his mission. He was living out the kind of dream many of us have, of being financially independent and with enough money to spread around for the betterment of the community. However, I did wonder what he would tell me, what he would add to what I already knew about verbal communication. As a professional communicator myself, and one who guided

34

others in that practice, I felt I was well versed in the process of getting the right message across.

AN OPEN MIND

All the same, I kept an open mind. There is always something new to learn, some new angle on an old belief. Otherwise there would never be any insight, any progress, any enlightenment. After all, it took something as tiny as an apple falling that led Newton to his theory of gravity, and a bath-time revelation that gave Archimedes his eureka moment. The more I thought along those lines, the more receptive I felt to the ideas of this unusual man.

Norman Sinclair then invited me to take notes if I wanted to, but added this caution: "Bear in mind that, while you are writing you are not listening, so please write down only the essentials. What I aim to do is to help you to a new understanding. If you understand what I share with you, it will change your approach. If you think differently, you will do differently. Does that make sense to you?"

I nodded and put my pen down. But I had a question: "Are you talking about business communication, as in presentation skills, or social conversation?"

"Good question," he replied. "Those are only different situations, not different kinds of communication. I'm concerned with the process of connecting the mind of the speaker with the mind of the listener. That process is relevant in conversations of all kinds, whether it's one-to-one or one-to-many, wouldn't you agree?" I nodded. "I want people to be more aware of the meaning of what they are communicating in their conversations. Good communication between individuals will create a more pleasant society. Good communication between political leaders will create a gentler, safer world. And the best place to start is with those you can influence yourself.

"I suppose you were wondering about my gifts to those rough sleepers in London? That's about my need to connect one-to-one with those I can help. As I said before, my pockets are not deep enough to solve the homelessness problem. Strange as it may seem, there will always be a number of street sleepers who will refuse the offer of a bed for the night. They have mental as well as financial problems and many of them fiercely resist any attempt to re-order their lives. I understand that. I accept it. And I try to do what I can by helping them in the place they have chosen for themselves.

"Local charities tell me when a person or a family is in desperate need of shelter, and I help if I can. But once a month I go up to London and wander about looking for people living on the streets, and I give them some money. It helps them in their immediate situations, and I like the connection. It's a different feeling from giving a cheque to a charity. I want sometimes to make a direct contribution to someone in need. Perhaps a mind doctor would analyse me and come up with an explanation, but there it is. And it's interesting that you should have seen me two months in a row. Maybe we were meant to connect. I hope so."

I was beginning to understand what he was trying to achieve. At least, I thought I was. However, I still wanted to know what my role would be in his grand plan. And yet, I have always welcomed unexpected encounters. You never know where they might lead, and often the outcome could be really rewarding. I decided to go along with it and see where it would lead me.

Chapter 3 Summary

About the lottery win

I drive to Norman's bungalow at Crockham Hill in Surrey.

Norman explains what he did with his big lottery win.
- Pockets not deep enough to solve homelessness
- Avoided wasted generosity to charities helping with distant disasters
- Focused on organisations helping improve communication

He blames social media for allowing or encouraging controversy to generate reader traffic.

His purpose is to improve relationships, on a personal level and also internationally, citing Brexit as one important example of the effect of bad communication. In contrast, he likes the direct contact with the homeless individuals he helps.

However, his focus is on understanding the process of communication – connecting the mind of the speaker with that of the listener.

Four

First truth of communication

In a soft, conversational tone, he casually enquired, "When you, as a speaker, want to improve your communication skills, where would you start? Where, in fact, did you start?"

"I joined Toastmasters International," I replied. "They have an exceptional programme for developing your public speaking skills. When I decided I wanted to be a speaker, that's where I went. In fact, quite a few people join Toastmasters when they have an important event in their lives which will require them to make a speech, for example when they are to be Best Man at a wedding, or when they have been elected Captain of the Golf Club."

"So you started by working on the way you organise your thoughts and put them across, is that right?"

"That's a fair summary. Yes, that's what I did, following their programme."

"Can you think of anything wrong with that process?"

I could see he was nudging me in a particular direction, but I wasn't sure where, or what he wanted me to say or think. So I just shrugged and said, "It's a good programme, tried and tested, and it helped me improve my skills in a structured way."

He nodded, indicating he understood what I was saying, but it was clearly not the answer he wanted, so I reversed the question and asked him what he thought was wrong with that.

"OK," he said, "let me ask you a different question. What is the essence of good communication? Is it having a simple message that you express clearly?"

That sounded like a fair definition, so I agreed.

ISOLATED ON AN ISLAND

"Well, I'm sure most people would agree with that. But let's change the environment. Let's place you, an accomplished speaker with a well-defined, simple message, able to express it clearly, using all the skills you developed at Toastmasters, let's place you on an uninhabited island in the middle of the Pacific. Can you visualise that?" I nodded, and he went on, "How much communication is possible? Let's suppose you stand on the beach and deliver your best speech. How effectively have you communicated?"

Now I could see where we were heading, and replied, "Obviously there has been no communication, because there is no one there to hear me."

"So you need a receiver, is that right?" I agreed. But he wasn't finished.

"Now imagine a bottle gets washed up on the beach. You find a leaf to write on and a twig that makes a mark and you write a message on the leaf, pop it into the bottle, seal it and throw in back in the water. How much communication now? You have composed your message and delivered it, but is that enough? And isn't that how many people communicate? They have something to say, they say it, and they consider the communication complete. Do you know anyone like that?"

I nodded. I knew lots of people, including professional speakers, who communicate that way. He continued.

"There's something missing, isn't there? As you said a moment ago, you need a Receiver. Eventually the bottle arrives on a beach in Japan, where a fisherman opens the bottle and sees your message. But you have written in English, and he cannot read that language. So you have a receiver, but he cannot understand your message, so how much communication have you achieved?"

His message was clear. For proper communication I needed a receiver who also understood what I was saying. And yet, said Norman, that was not the complete answer. "The first truth about effective communication," he said, "and you can write this down: **the first truth is that communication is not about Transmission, it's about Reception**. It's about how it is received and understood.

Toastmasters and other training programmes may help you develop your skill in putting your thoughts together and then putting them across, but that's not the whole story. Let's take a sideways step first.

HAMILTON'S POSTULATE

"When I started thinking about having this conversation with someone like you, my focus was on the communication process in business and in serious exchanges between two people. But I realised that even those small, casual greetings in passing can have an effect on relationships. My Logic lecturer at university used to speak about a logician called Hamilton, whose Postulate states: *It is permissible to state (or address) explicitly in language what is implicitly contained in the thought.*

"Here's one example: Suppose you ask me if it's OK to walk across my grass. I hesitate for a moment, then reply, *It's OK.* In my mind I have considered the effect of denying you permission and decided the damage you do to my grass is repairable and less important than the effect on our relationship if I am inflexible. But you notice my hesitation, understand what it means and act accordingly, by walking around the grass. You have made explicit my unspoken desire to deny you permission and acted on it. And there has been a reciprocal transfer of courtesies, first from me, in not saying No, and then from you in not offending me.

"The problem is, we might surmise incorrectly what is contained in the thought behind the words. In that example, my hesitation might have been because I did not want your shoes to get muddy by walking on the path around the grass. Despite your good intentions you might have walked on the path, got muddy shoes, which you then trampled into my house. So, after a quick assessment, I might have decided it was better for you to walk on the grass.

"As recently as the late '90s someone published **The Language of Thought Hypothesis**, or LOTH in short. It postulated that thought and the process of thinking take place in a mental language, which they said was a symbolic system that represents attitudes. This idea is central to what I am talking about. Here's a very simple example. Person A likes person B. When person A thinks of person B, he or she knows or feels that liking. That positive connection, that *liking,* is the language of thought. Words can then be used to explain or articulate that thought.

"Before I say any more about that, let's go right back to basics. How do we humans differ from all other beings on this planet? We speak. We have language. And that language is much more than a collection of sounds. Animals and birds have language too. But our language is different. It enables us to communicate what is in our minds and in our hearts. It allows us to communicate abstract concepts, even thoughts of things that do not actually exist.

"Animals have feelings too and can express them in their behaviour, but they lack the kind of verbal language that human have. Can they be taught it? Yes they can. Koko was a Lowland Gorilla who was taught sign language and mastered 1,100 words. She could look in a mirror and "say" *That's me.* She could sign, *You tickle*

43

and before she died she signed, *But man stupid. Must save the Earth.* That's a pretty abstract thought!

"Returning to LOTH, at the root of the things I say there might be a thought such as *I believe this* or *I want this.* There will then be a causal connection with your response. In other words, I will be prompting your reply or your reaction, because I want you to agree with me or to adopt the proposition I am putting to you.

THOUGHT'S MEANING & INTENTION

"LOTH seems to extend the earlier work done on the notion of Mental Representation. A thought has meaning and intention. But also, the validity of anything I say depends on the validity of the empirical evidence. I can say or claim anything, but I cannot expect you to accept or believe it unless I can offer you the evidence to prove it. For example, whether I call you dogmatic or flexible, I must be able to define what I mean by the terms dogmatic or flexible, and point to examples of how you match that definition.

"In contrast, consider how some people utter clichés, mantras and dogmas without understanding them. They assume that the words they speak convey an inherent truth, a truth that has not originated as an idea in their own minds. They think that it's enough to utter a statement to make it true. They said it, therefore it is so. And that is one of the causes of miscommunication which we should seek to eliminate. Why is this relevant and why should we try to understand and manage our semantics?

"Our communication style can shape our relationships, even without our knowledge, and we can unconsciously convey a message we did not intend. Poor communication can result in lost business or personal relationships going sour. So let me focus on coping with the problems that can arise through poor communication styles, as well as how to get your point across in the best possible way. As many clever people have said, your conversational style can make or break relationships.

"I'll come to that in a little while."

Norman paused, to give me a chance to take in what he had said. He stood up and helped himself to a glass of water, calling out to me from across the room. He said that although his focus was on the effect of communication on relationships, he was interested in how professional speakers like me tackled the subject. He asked me to tell him about my own speeches.

I said, "First let me tell you of an exchange I had on Facebook with a friend of mine, Judith. She calls herself a socialised maverick. I asked her if it matters how you argue a point, so long as you can prove the 'truth' of your point of view. I said I found that some mavericks have a contentious or argumentative style that is counter-persuasive, and which could get in the way of effective communication. They raise hackles, so their point is not readily accepted.

"In reply Judith said that for her the message is more important than the delivery. And then she threw in an unexpected element. She said that people who resist a contentious style may have fragile egos. To me she seemed to be saying that if communication failed because on the speaker's argumentative style, the fault would lie with the recipient, because they had a fragile ego.

"TRANSMISSION DEPENDS ON VALID CONTENT"

"You were saying, Norman, that the first truth of communication is that communication is about Reception, not Transmission. Judith said content mattered more than delivery. To be clear, she was talking about the style of delivery. She was saying that Transmission depended on valid content, and that the style of delivery was less important. I take it you would not agree?"

Norman thought for a moment, then replied, "She's not wrong, in one sense. Yes, the content is more important than the manner of delivery. So, on an academic level, that is right. However, in the context of interpersonal communication, what matters more than the content is the way in which it is received. You can be absolutely right about something you say, but if you antagonise your listener your communication will fail. And it will fail for a reason that has nothing to do with the validity of your message. It will fail for a reason that has nothing to do with your command of the spoken language. It will fail because of your attitude, because your attitude has got in the way of whatever you intended to put across.

"This is the very point I am trying to make: communicate with a purpose. And do so in a way that will get your listeners on side. Otherwise it becomes a shouting match in which each person hopes to win the argument by making the loudest noise. But let's now return to your role in all this, and why I wanted especially to talk to you about it."

Chapter 4 Summary

First truth about communication

We talked about the essence of good communication. Was it having a simple message, expressed clearly?

Norman then asked me to consider the example of someone alone on an uninhabited island, and how that person would communicate. He said the listener would play a vital part. Taking a sideways step, he asked me to consider the meaning of Hamilton's Postulate and how we address the hidden meaning.

The Language of Thought Hypothesis (LOTH) similarly focuses on the attitude behind what we say. We can express that because we have mutual understanding and a language that can do that, unlike the more limited language of animals and birds.

Our communication style, said Norman, can make or break relationships. On the interpersonal level, what matters more than content is the way it is received. Attitude can get in the way.

The First Truth is that communication is not about Transmission; it's about the way it is received & understood.

Five

Second truth of communication

"Before we talk about your role, let me address the second vital truth of communication," said Norman. "And this is central to the whole conversation you and I are having. It is also pivotal in understanding the process of conveying our thoughts and ideas to one another.

"The vital truth is this: **do not speak to be understood. Speak to avoid being misunderstood**.

"You have heard that said before. So have I. It's not an original thought. But it's one of the most important thoughts for anyone who ever tries to explain ideas to other people. It is central to the way we speak to one another, to the way we express ourselves, to the success of leadership, and it is how to avoid many of the crossed lines in diplomatic exchanges.

"Consider the consequences of being misunderstood. One of the best-known examples was the Charge of the

Light Brigade during the Crimean War's Battle of Balaclava. It was an infamous incident immortalised in a poem by Alfred, Lord Tennyson. The British commander Lord Raglan intended to send the Light Brigade to retrieve guns from the overrun Turkish positions, but his messenger, Captain Louis Edward Nolan, indicated the wrong enemy guns with a wide sweep of his arm.

SOMEONE HAD BLUNDERED

"Lord Lucan, commander of the British cavalry, then instructed his brother-in-law, Lord Cardigan (whom he disliked), to lead his 670 troopers "into the valley of death". As Tennyson memorably put it, "someone had blundered" and two-thirds of the Light Brigade were wiped out.

"Captain Nolan was at fault and would have been court martialed had he survived. He delivered an imprecise order verbally instead of handing over the written order. He did not check that the order had been clearly understood. And it played into the prickly relationship between Lucan and Cardigan. The disastrous Charge of the Light Brigade is still quoted by military analysts as an example of what can go wrong when orders are unclear.

"First an example involving the Americans: the Massacre at Wounded Knee. In 1890, the US Government mistakenly believed that the revival of a traditional dance by Native Americans indicated they were working towards an uprising, and Chief Sitting Bull was shot dead by policemen at the Standing Rock Reservation. It worsened relations between the Native Americans and the White Man. Two weeks later, a US army unit intercepted a band of Sioux who were on their way to the Pine Ridge Reservation. They demanded that the Sioux hand over their weapons. Most complied but one was deaf and held on to his rifle, saying it was expensive. In the struggle a shot was accidentally fired, the soldiers thought they were under attack and opened fire on the unarmed tribe, killing 250 of them. It was one of the worst massacres in American history.

"Much more common are examples of culture clashes. A Scandinavian engineer was sent out to India to teach a client company's engineers how to operate a new technical system. Adopting a Western management practice, he decided to instruct the local Chief Engineer, who could then train his team. At each stage of his instruction he asked, *Do you understand?* And of course the Indian Chief Engineer said Yes. When the process was over, the Scandinavian summoned the whole team and told them the Chief Engineer was going to explain it all to them.

"It was a disaster, and the Chief Engineer lost face. When he'd been asked if he understood, he could not say No. That would have meant either that he was slow to understand or that the foreigner had failed as a teacher. He said Yes out of politeness. The Scandinavian engineer applied his own (Western) expectations, and got it badly wrong.

HEARING WHAT THEY EXPECTED

"Let's consider how those several misunderstandings arose. In each of those examples, there was a predisposition to accept the norm of their peers, to

51

accept what turned out to be the wrong interpretation. Therefore there was no inclination to check.

"At Balaclava the Light Brigade was primed and ready for action, just awaiting orders. In other words, just expecting someone to press the button. As a military man and an aristocrat schooled in deference to lines of command, Lord Lucan was programmed to follow orders and, when they came, he did not consider challenging them. Nor could he be bothered conferring with Lord Cardigan, because they disliked each other. Message received. Carry on. Just following orders.

"At Wounded Knee, the background was the tension caused by the misunderstanding that led to Chief Sitting Bull being shot by policemen. Then, in the scuffle to seize the last rifle from the Sioux Indians, the US soldiers were on high alert, expecting retaliation. When you expect retaliation, you will see or hear it in every response.

"And finally, the Scandinavian Engineer had meant well. He thought he was boosting the Indian Chief Engineer by inviting him to pass on what he had learned. That would have been the norm in Scandinavia. He did not understand how Indians receive instruction.

"Now what did those three examples have in common? In every instance, the interpretation was based on what was expected, not on what was intended. You may remember that earlier I said communication is not about transmission, but rather on how it is received and understood. That's the first principle of communication. This is the reverse of the same coin. It's about avoiding being misunderstood, because people have their own predispositions in place, and those will filter what you say to fit what they expect to hear.

"Let's talk for a moment about filters. We have our own filters in place, and those will colour what we say. And what we say will then be altered as they pass through the filters of those who hear what we say. Those filters start with our vocabulary and the way our community normally says things. A nation's language reflects its thinking style. This matters very much in communicating across cultures, especially in East-West dialogue.

DIFFERENT COMMUNICATION STYLES

"Here's a simple example. Suppose you asked your wife, *Is my dinner not yet ready?* If she is English, she would probably answer *No,* i.e. *No, it's not ready yet.* But if she were Chinese, she would more likely reply, *Yes,* meaning *Yes, it's not yet ready.*

"The broad difference between East and West in communication styles is that the West uses logic and argument to get others to agree, whereas the East prefers to influence through harmony and peer pressure, appealing to the emotions. Deborah Tannen, in her book, *You Just Don't Understand,* says that there is a similar difference between men and women. Men will seek to gain acceptance of what they say, but women are more likely to appeal to your emotions and seek to influence you. Male experts will assume the role of lecturer, whereas women will seek rapport and play down their expertise rather than display it.

"It doesn't matter whether the difference is East-West or male-female, there will always be two different points of view when two people's paths cross. So there will always be a conflict of interest, both in the points of view being expressed and in the preferred outcome. And that's when we come to consider the intention of the communication.

"First, a generalisation. Deborah Tannen says women use language to express rapport, men do so for self-display. That's a broad statement about the usual verbal style of women and men, and I suppose she means western people, or those in the western culture. Clearly traditional orientals might have a different style.

"Perhaps it would be useful to consider how couples communicate, and why they often get it wrong. Couples set aside some of the usual social politeness, so we can see the unvarnished miscues. Here's a common example:

"Wife says, *On our way home, let's drop in to see my sister.*
"Husband replies, *What for?*
"Wife says, *OK, we don't have to go there.*

UNDERLYING ATTITUDE

"She then goes silent for the rest of the journey home and remains distant all evening. Her husband doesn't notice at first, then thinks she's just in one of her moods. But let's deconstruct that little dialogue. When Husband asks *What for?*, he means, *Is there some special reason? Something I should know about?* He is just asking for a bit more info. But Wife hears, *I'd rather not go there.* Perhaps it even reminds her that he doesn't really like her sister, which is why they don't see much of her. Her resentment builds up, but it is based on a false assumption. And over time, that results in two obstacles to a clear connection between them: first, the cumulative resentment about his apparent resistance to what she wants, and secondly, she will instinctively avoid making such suggestions in future.

"What's the answer? It lies in developing the right attitude. If the wife suspects there might be resistance to a suggestion, she could build in a get-out clause for her husband. She could say, for example, *Do you mind if we drop in to see my sister for a moment?* He should be sensitive to her wishes and agree, or else explain why he would rather not. If he wants more information, he should simply ask for it. It all hinges on caring enough about each other to avoid being misunderstood.

"That's the starting point for getting it right – a small but very significant step. The US Admiral William H. McRaven says, *If you wanna change the world, start off by making your bed. When you make your bed you will have accomplished the first task of the day.*"

Chapter 5 Summary

Second truth of communication

Do not speak to be understood. Rather speak to avoid being misunderstood.

Examples of catastrophes resulting from miscommunication include The Charge of the Light Brigade and the Massacre at Wounded Knee. What was intended and what was heard were different, largely because of what the listener in each case expected to hear.

Misunderstandings can also occur because of cultural differences, as with the Scandinavian engineer who caused his Indian counterpart to lose face, and the different ways some nations use the English language. They might arise between couples because of built-up resentments. Much depends on developing the right attitude.

Corrections need to be built up one small step at a time.

Six

Third truth of communication

"There is a third truth," said Norman. "I referred to it earlier. It's the element that probably matters most of all. It depends on how you make the receiver feel. Never forget that your receiver, your listener, plays an important part in the communication process."

Norman placed his laptop before me and opened up Facebook. He showed me a dialogue between two professional speakers that illustrated an important point about the language we use, and its effect on one another. The thread opened with a poster that stated, "If everyone in the audience likes my performance, then I failed."

In the comments that followed, one contributor wrote, "I think deliberately intending to make people disagree is unprofessional." The person who started the thread responded with, "Thanks for the personal attack." Norman asked for my reaction to the exchange.

I said, "The problem lies with the word *unprofessional*. If you describe a behaviour as unprofessional, it will ALWAYS be considered an attack on the person who did the behaviour. Some words have that effect.

"That's exactly right," said Norman, "And that's why I showed you that Facebook thread. The language you use can produce an effect you did not intend. There are some people who contend that they can criticise an action without intending to criticise the person, and parents often say you may condemn the behaviour but not the child. I'm not so sure. When you admonish people for what they have done, be they adult or child, they will always feel personally criticised. So what's the answer? I'm not saying you should not disagree, judge or criticise what someone else says or does. But I am asking you to consider the effect of your words and decide if you are happy with the likely outcome. Always think about how you will make the other person feel about what you say to them."

RIGHT AUDIENCE?

I said I agreed. In fact, I recalled a speech contest which I thought I'd won, but in which I was ranked second. At the end of the contest, quite a few members of the audience lined up to congratulate me on my performance. One man said, "Don't be disheartened. Best speech, wrong audience."

I thought about that comment. A lot. Why was it the wrong audience? It was an American audience of about 2,000, and my speech opened with a quote from Invictus, by William Henley. In fact, the theme was "bloody but unbowed", a message of fighting back against life's travails. Although the message was pretty much in line with motivational speeches familiar to Toastmasters, even as I dwelt on William Henley's ordeal of having his feet amputated with only Listerine as an anaesthetic, lauding his *grit*, I knew I was winning the admiration of the audience, but not their hearts. The language of the poem itself, which I quoted in part, pitched the speech beyond a visceral appeal, with lines like, *In the fell clutch of circumstance I have not winced nor cried aloud, Under the bludgeoning of chance my head is bloody but unbowed.*

The winner had a simpler message, based on the film of *Beauty and the Beast*. Even I felt the rising tension in the room as he sang the villagers' ruthless song in a strong bass baritone, ending with, "We'll kill the beast!!" A moment's pause, then a shrug and a puzzled, "Why?" At this the audience bellowed their release from the tension, and that was the moment he won the judges' verdict. It was all about who had better connected with the audience, not who had the better text. It was about how we made them feel.

This, I said to Norman, is especially important in business presentations. If the message were enough, you could mail your presentation and wait for the orders to flood in. Clearly that would not work. So what can a presenter add in person? It's that connection with the hearts of the hearers, it's about managing the way they feel about the message.

Norman nodded, adding, "I think it's well known that almost everyone buys on emotion and justifies with reason."

"Yes," I replied, "that's why you sell the benefits not the features. More importantly, you sell your product or service as the way to cure, remove or prevent some pain. The clever sales person starts by asking the sort of questions that will bring out that pain and emphasise the damage it is doing. That's when the prospect will say, or think, *I do want to take care of that.* That's the emotional appeal."

Norman agreed, but he wanted to return to the way we express ourselves, especially when we want the other person to do something they may not have considered doing. He asked me, "What was your first impression on this house when you arrived this morning?"

I said, "It was the location. I loved the way it fitted so well into the environment, its seclusion, and the magnificent view."

"Shall I tell you what made me decide to buy it? The estate agent brought me here, made me a cup of tea and sat me down in a chair facing the view you admired. He then invited me to spend an hour or so in the house on my own, while he went about his business. In that hour I was able to imagine myself living here, enjoying the view, feeling safe in its seclusion, relishing the sense of owning all this. When he returned he did not have to tell me anything about the benefits of this house. It had already made me feel it was my home. He had allowed me to make my own decision about the way I felt about this house.

"How we feel about a product or service will often override such considerations as price. In our local town there is a shop that sells expensive chocolates. That's where you'd go to get a gift for your hostess when you've been invited for dinner. There's a card stating that the beautifully decorated chocolates are hand-made, and there are 15 or 20 different designs. You pick the ones you want, and they are carefully placed in a golden box, and you get two layers! Then the box is gift wrapped with a ribbon, and the whole presentation is so attractive, you never even notice the price.

EMOTIONAL APPEAL

It's all designed to make you feel almost grateful for the wonderful present they are putting together for you to take to your hostess. They are not selling you a box of chocolates. They are constructing a beautiful gift on your behalf. That's about providing a service in order to make a sale. Providing the service makes the prospect feel good about buying your product or service."

I could see the sense of that, but a thought occurred to me about the greater significance of what Norman was telling me. Could the kind of thinking that lies behind the principles of communication, and the third principle in particular, be applied to other activities, such as selling? I had a presentation to prepare, pitching for a sales training contract, and I needed some new thinking to add to what I already knew.

Norman said, "I once knew a man who had just started selling life assurance and was having difficulty finding prospects. One day he met an insurance broker – this was before we started doing everything online -- who arranged motor insurance, but didn't handle very much life assurance.

" Knowing that car insurance clients tended to shop around and change providers almost every year, he offered to go through the customer record cards and update them, if he could also offer them life assurance. The broker agreed. Updating the client records was an important task that he didn't have spare staff to carry out. So the rookie life assurance salesman went through the record cards, calling up past clients saying, *We looked after your car insurance in the past. Did we ever help you build up a lump sum for the future? Would you find it useful if I came and showed you how to do that?* " He very quickly cleaned up the client list and sold a lot of endowment policies. Private pension plans too. He didn't just ask for access to the broker's clients. That would have been self-serving. Instead, he offered to do something useful for the broker. It was an offer that would benefit both of them.

"What did that have in common with what we have been talking about? Simply this: whether you are making a speech, a presentation or simply a verbal proposition, you need to think about what will make your proposition persuasive. And often its isn't your proposition itself, but what you say and do *before* you make your pitch, that will put the other person in a receptive frame of mind. The brilliant Robert Cialdini has writing a book about that. It's called *Pre-Suasion*. He calls it a revolutionary way to influence and persuade. But it's simply about the way you make people feel even before you say a word."

Chapter 6 Summary

Third truth of communication

Successful communication depends on how you make your listener feel.

The language you use can override your intention, so always think about the likely effect of the words you use. Some words will always be considered pejorative, and some vocabulary might evoke admiration, but fail to reach the hearts of your hearers.

Remember that people buy on emotion and justify with reason, so to be more persuasive you should first aim to make your listeners or prospects feel good. That's what Robert Cialdini calls Pre-suasion. For example, make a generous offer before asking for anything, and focus on giving rather than taking.

THE MAN WHO GAVE AWAY HIS LOTTERY WIN

Seven

Five Questions

Norman said, "Just for a moment, let's focus on professional speakers and the special considerations that apply to the speeches they make from conference platforms and in training sessions. What about your own professional speech, what does it say about you? Yes, you know what your message is, but have you thought about what it says about you, the speaker? Take a moment to think about the mindset that created it. How well does it serve you? Is that an idea worth considering?"

It was a valid question, or series of questions, and it chimed well with my own thoughts about public speaking. I said, "I think you're right. I believe many speakers travel on a false assumption. It's what I call Better Mousetrap thinking. I think it was Ralph Waldo Emerson who said that if you build a better mousetrap the world will beat a path to your door. It's the illusion that if you get very good at what you do, people will

65

come looking for you. They will not. You need something else."

Norman said, "And what would that be?"

"Have you heard of the Nook?" I asked him. "It's an e-reader developed by Barnes & Noble, America's largest bookseller. At the very start they claimed it surpassed the Kindle in every way, but it's always been second best to Kindle. And why? Because it's just an individual product that doesn't strongly connect with the way readers run their lives.

OUR BUYING ECOSYSTEM

"People develop habits. They go to Google for info, Apple for computers or mobile phones, eBay for bargains, Amazon for digital stuff and books. If they are looking for books online, their starting point is Amazon and books from Amazon are available on Kindle. An article in Forbes called that habit an ecosystem. The Nook has to compete with that well-developed habit. It is a good product, but it has to be positioned where people habitually go to buy books. That's the first level. Amazon first, Kindle second. The Nook always ranks below Kindle because it is competing at the level of the second decision – they are expecting people to start with them. But they are not the first port of call for books. Amazon is.

"Here's an example of another wrong focus. Earlier this year, an independent business consultant told me he'd been invited to apply for a high-level job with a large insurance company that needed a boost. He was asked to deliver a 15-minute presentation about himself at the start of the interview, and asked for my help. I asked what he planned to tell them. He recited a litany of his many skills and successes over the past ten years or so. His outline presentation was a version of his CV. How do you think that improved his chances?

"I told him, don't think of yourself as a job applicant. I said, you're a consultant. Why not think of yourself as the consultant called in to revive a stagnant company? How would you go about it? He said, *I'd start by asking questions to find out what the problem was and why they had a problem. That's what I usually do.* And he spoke with enthusiasm about how he would go about the revival.

"It was so different from his original approach. So we started again. I asked him, what's the insurance company's mission statement? He didn't know. I asked what he thought it should be, and after a bit of trial and error, we arrived at this: *The pursuit of excellence in the service of the customer.*

"That is what he believed the company should be focused on. That became the theme of his presentation. Not himself, not his CV, but rather what the insurance company should be aiming to achieve, and how he would help them to get there. His work history simply listed what he had done in the past. But *how* he had done it defined his Added Value. That's where needed to focus.

THE EXPERT'S DILEMMA

"That consultant's dilemma is echoed by many speakers. There are speakers who wonder if they are on the right track, there are speakers who promote themselves as experts in their subjects, and get no takers, there are speakers who get gigs but don't get asked back. Like the consultant, they haven't worked out their Added Value.

"I asked myself what such speakers are saying about themselves. Are they saying, *Listen to me, I'm an expert*? How would you react if someone said that to you? So what's the answer? It starts with your sense of purpose. Imagine you were starting your speaking career from scratch. What would you speak about? What do you know that will be of benefit to others?

"The first question to answer is, **what's your Added Value?** Are you someone who is expert in a subject and speaks about it, or are you the walking problem solver, the thought leader on that subject? Do you speak to impress, or to inspire?"

I told Norman about one of the most impressive speeches on YouTube. Back in 2006, Sir Ken Robinson gave a TED talk asking if schools kill creativity. It has had over 16 million views. One of the largest number of hits for a YouTube clip. And why? Did he present himself as an expert in education? No. He talked about the loss to society of the creative genius that lies in every school child, and which is educated out of them by career-related knowledge.

In one of my own speeches, aimed at other speakers, I talk about a simple formula that consists of 5 little questions that they should apply to themselves, as an analysis of their speeches. They will help to re-focus their mindset and the way they approach their listeners. The five questions are:

- Why?
- Why not?
- What?
- So what?
- What next?

Those questions are easy to remember. What's my purpose? It's to move speakers away from delivering information and towards problem solving. I tell them: just remember, people don't care about what you know. They only care about the benefit of what you know. You must have the right focus. I take them through my five questions.

FIVE ESSENTIAL QUESTIONS

<u>QUESTION ONE</u> is: WHY? That means, why am I here?

When I was training a team of classified advertising sales people, I told them to go past the obvious answers like, "I'm here to make a sale". That's like saying a taxi driver is in business to offer you a ride in his car. He's not. He's in business to get you to your destination in comfort. So consider your business purpose. I said, you are in business to enable advertisers to find candidates for the jobs they had to fill, or to sell their houses or holidays. You are not in business to sell advertising. You are in business to help advertisers to achieve their own purposes.

I challenge professional speakers saying, What about you? What business are you in? As a speaker, you are in business to help your listeners achieve their own goals, solve their problems, improve their lot in life. Don't think of yourself as an expert who speaks. That focuses on you. Think of yourself as a problem solver. Problem solving is why you are addressing that audience.

QUESTION TWO follows on from that. It's: WHY NOT?

My advertising sales people sometimes had a crisis of confidence and asked themselves, Why should they see me? Similarly, as a speaker, you may wonder why your audiences should listen to you. But I say, why not? Here's why not. Our advertisers had a need. They needed to find candidates for the jobs they wanted to fill. They didn't want to see us just to enjoy our company. They had a real need, and we could help them meet that need. That's why they had to see us.

I tell speakers, the same applies to you. Your listeners have needs and they are expecting that you might have the answers to those needs. Don't be a supplicant, don't seek the permission, approval or applause of the audience. Be like a doctor. If someone has an illness, they want to see the doctor. Think about the consequence of NOT seeing the doctor! Think what happens to a sick person who refuses to see a doctor. Therefore, the answer to the Why Not question is this: because you have the answer to their needs.

QUESTION THREE is: WHAT?

This is the key question. What are you offering? What's your Unique Selling Proposition, your USP? When I was at the Daily Express, we were competing with the Daily Telegraph for job advertising. Both papers had similar readers, but the Telegraph was the market leader. Better paper, better market place. But you had to wait to get your ad published. We could publish the ad tomorrow. That made us different – the first step in a USP.

Not only that. I offered a reward for anyone who found their job through the Daily Express. I actively brought readers and advertisers together. No other newspaper was doing that. That was my Added Value. That gave my ad salesmen two distinctions to offer: one, a quicker solution to the advertiser's needs, and two, readers who were motivated to respond. Those two elements made our proposition different from and better than the market leader.

Did it work? Well, in today's terms, our ad revenue went from £10 million to £30 million in ten months.

So how can you make your proposition distinctive? How can you distinguish yourself from other speakers offering a similar message? Here are two things that can make you different and better. First, you have something that no one else has. It's your point of view. It's your 'take' on the subject. That is the filter through which your content has to pass.

The second difference is this: don't speak about what you know, speak about the benefit of what you know. Speak to the hearts of your hearers. That is your Added Value.

QUESTION FOUR is SO WHAT?

That means, "Why are you telling me this?" My ad salesmen were often afraid to ask for the order. So what was the purpose of their presentations? I told them, when you have made your case and got acceptance, you have to ask for the order. Why? Because of the value of your proposition. The value to <u>them</u>.

I say, as a speaker you first have to identify the needs of your listeners, then build their interest in your solution to the point where they want it. And what do you do then? I'll tell you what many speakers do. They say Thank you, and sit down. Why? The purpose of your speech has to be to bring about some change. That's why you have to tell them what to do next to bring about that change, and make it easy.

<u>QUESTION FIVE</u> is about Relationship building. The question is, WHAT NEXT?

I told my ad salesmen to stop thinking of every pitch as a Yes/No binary situation and think instead of building a relationship. If now was not the right time for an order, they had to leave the door open. Speakers could end their speeches by offering a follow-up session, a Part Two, or a training day, or even a request for a referral. They should always think of The Next Step. Without a Next Step much of what they have said will be wasted. The Next Step is about putting into practice the lessons in their speeches. And The Next Step provides the reason for further contact, for a continuing relationship.

THE SPEAKER'S RELEVANCE

To summarise, those five questions will help speakers establish their relevance, their true purpose:

- **Why?** That's your real purpose in being there.

- **Why not?** That's about understanding that they have needs that you could satisfy.
- **What?** That's the Added Value you are offering.
- **So what?** That's the purpose of your speech and what they should do with it.
- **What next?** That's leaving the door open. It's the next step.

I usually finish that part of the speech with, "When you have understood that your purpose is to help solve the problems of your listeners, you will speak to inspire not to impress."

At the end of my speech I will say, "I do not ask you to make great speeches. I ask you to make *every* speech with great care – care for the needs and aspirations of your listeners, care for the good that you can do for them, care for the change that you can help to bring about. Make it a change for the better."

If Norman had not expected such a detailed answer, he gave no sign of it. In fact, he seemed to think it fitted well with what he was going to tell me. After all, he did say it was my turn next!

Chapter 7 Summary

FIVE QUESTIONS

Understand that people develop habits and their buying decisions follow an ecosystem. That explains why a product that is superior to the market leader may never overtake it.

Norman Sinclair asks my views on where professional speakers should focus.

I mention Better Mousetrap thinking and why The Nook will always lag behind Kindle. The speakers' dilemma is whether to speak about their expertise or their Added Value.

Five questions will help speakers establish their relevance, the answer to their dilemma.

1. *Why?* Your real purpose for being on the stage.
2. *Why not?* Understanding that your listeners have needs
   that you could satisfy.
3. *What?* The Added Value you are offering.
4. *So what?* The purpose of your speech and what your listeners
   should do with it.
5. *What next?* Leaving the door open. It's the next step.

THE MAN WHO GAVE AWAY HIS LOTTERY WIN

Eight

Getting Acceptance

Norman was silent for a long moment, then he said, "That's a great way to help speakers understand their true purpose. And not just speakers. It's relevant to anyone who uses persuasion – sales people, marketers, advertisers, those in PR, even journalists."

He stood up and walked around the room while he took in what I'd said about my five questions, then returned to sit again directly in front of me, to maintain eye contact, but he did not sit too close, respecting my personal space bubble. His energy was up, and when he started speaking he was immediately in full flow. Clearly he was passionate about the topic of our conversation, but it was equally apparent that he relished the chance to share his thinking with someone who might become his collaborator in spreading his ideas on better communication.

I had a thought and stopped him to ask a question I had asked before. "Are we talking about business communication, Norman, or will this be also relevant to social conversations? Surely that has a bearing on what we do to gain acceptance of what we say?"

"Good question," he replied, and I'm glad you asked it. We both know that there are thousands of books on speaking better, on sales presentations, on overcoming the fear of public speaking, and so many other topics about verbal communication. The two questions we should be addressing right now are, A. How is this different? And B. Are we addressing a business audience or a lay one? I think your question was B, wasn't it?"

"Yes, that's right. Who is the audience?"

THE PUBLIC IS NOT YOUR AUDIENCE

"Then let me start with Question B: you may remember I touched on this at the start of our conversation this morning, when you first asked that question. My intention is to address the person who wants to connect better with the person he or she is talking to," he said carefully. "That person could be in a social context or it could be a business one, and it could also be in a political arena. Whether that person is speaking informally to one other person, or formally to a large audience, what I am talking about will be equally relevant. If we have the right understanding about the process of communication – interpersonal communication – we'll get it right in a business situation as well as in a personal encounter.

"Here's a general principle about target groups: the public is not your audience; the public *contains* your audience. It's the principle that guides all forms of marketing and it applies to every person or organisation that is in the business of providing a solution to a need or a problem. However universal your solution may be, if you aim at the entire population, you will fail. That's a scatter-gun approach. Aim only at those who, *at this moment in time*, have a need for what you are offering.

"And what exactly am I offering? A clearer understanding of the process of verbal communication, of the means by which we share our ideas and our thinking with those whom we seek to influence. And why? Because that process is not properly understood, it is widely misused, and it causes too many of the world's serious problems. Starting with you, and eventually through you and those with whom you might share these ideas, I'd like to start a series of dialogues that prompt people to stop and think about the impact and the consequences of what they say and learn to say it differently.

"Question A was: how is this different from all those books on communication skills, the collected wisdom of all those speakers and trainers who have followed in the footsteps of Dale Carnegie, Zig Ziglar, Tony Robbins and the like? As you will gather, it is different in two ways. One, it is just common sense, not technical. And two, its focus is not on putting your point across. It is about understanding how you are being received and understood, and successfully managing that process to gain acceptance of your ideas.

"For example, have a look at all the training programmes on communication skills. What proportion of those courses is on listening skills? Small. And when you examine the content of listening skills, what do you find? Eye contact, posture, body language, repeating what you have just heard, and so on. All valid, but these are techniques. And they are not central to the skill of listening as part of the process of communicating. The central idea has to be understanding what's behind what is being said. Understanding why the other person is saying what he or she is saying, and why he or she is saying it in that way.

"The elements I'd like to discuss with you concern the process of transmission and reception, the two-way process that connects the thinking and intentions of both parties. Let's construct a scenario that will make it easy for people to remember and reconstruct some of the essential elements of communication. Do you agree that your recall of ideas or information is helped by using vivid images?"

18TH CENTURY COURTIER

I nodded. It's a well-trodden path for remembering things.

"I want you to imagine an 18th century scene in England. There's a crisis in the kingdom and a courtier has been sent to the king to persuade him to release more resources to overcome the problem. He has to observe all the courtesies of the time, present his credentials, get to the point quickly without being prescriptive, and use language that allows the king to believe it's all his own decision. Finally, he has to leave the king feeling good about his decision. Can you visualise the courtier and the scene? Describe in detail what you see in your mind's eye."

"I think I can," I said, as the image sharpened in my mind. "I see a chap in a yellow knee-length coat, over an embroidered waistcoat, with a white silk shirt and a cravat. He's wearing knee breeches, white silk stockings, black buckle shoes with 2-inch heels, and a barrister's wig under a three-cornered hat with upturned brim which, of course, he will remove when before the king. Oh, and he's carrying a walking stick with a silver grip. I'd say he's nervous about addressing the king who is known to be temperamental, so he takes some time to prepare what he's going to say."

"Pretty good," said Norman, "but what happens when the courtier returns home?"

"Oh yes," I added, "He writes a note of thanks to the king, summarising what was agreed between them. That follow-up is vital."

"Great! And here again are 5 important things that happened in that little scenario:

1. First he prepared. He worked out his opening, recognising that the impact of his first few words would determine whether the king would listen to him.
2. Then he thought about the language he would use and its structure, bearing in mind the difference between informative content and persuasive language, and taking care to avoid being misunderstood.
3. Next came his style of delivery. He had to be direct at first, getting quickly to the point, but he had also to be indirect, diplomatic, hinting at the desired solution and allowing the king to take ownership of the idea.
4. He made the king feel good about the exchange. That was the emotional connection, the vital step that made the king want to provide the solution.
5. Finally, he followed up. That was the essential Next Step.

"Let's talk about those elements in the communication process," he said. "They are not in any particular order, and they will not always be present when you communicate, and some may be more relevant to business communication than ordinary conversations, but that scenario with the courtier in the 1700s will help your memory of the 5 essential elements. First on the list was The Effect on the Listener. The courtier, or

80

Messenger, first had to consider the effect his message was likely to have on the king. I learned something about that when I joined Blackheath Harriers.

DIDN'T KNOW IT WAS A PUT DOWN

"I was living in Bromley at the time," he continued, "and I joined the Blackheath Harriers in Hayes. The club originated in Blackheath, hence its name, but it moved to Hayes many years ago. The first event I ran in was the annual Handicap race at the start of the winter season. It worked a little like the handicaps in golf, to enable all to compete on more equal terns. As a newcomer with no previous form, I was given the largest handicap. When the race was over, I showered, changed and went home. Then the phone rang. It was the Winter Captain asking me to return to the clubhouse because I had won the Handicap race! So back I went and sat among the diners until it was time for the awards.

"The Club Chairman was a man with limited social skills, which soon became obvious. He was in the role almost on a Buggins' Turn basis. As a long-time member, it was his turn to be in the chair, and he had no other obvious qualifications for the role. I've never forgotten how he announced my award: *The winner of the Handicap race was someone who had the maximum handicap.* I don't think for one moment that he had any malicious intent, but he had no idea that his announcement, expressed in that way, was a put-down. It diminished any sense of achievement I might have had, and reduced the value of the tankard I was given. One of the senior members of the club noticed the gaffe, and its effect must have showed on my face. He later told me to pay no attention to the man. *He doesn't know any better,* he said.

"What I learned from that incident was always to take account of the possible impact on others of the things we say, to think about how our words may be misconstrued or misunderstood, to be aware of how they are received. It taught me to avoid using language that is ambiguous, or at least to be alert to that possibility.

"Staying with the subject of the effect on others, you may remember that the Duke of Edinburgh is famous, or infamous, for shooting from the lip. At the turn of the year 2018, on his way to church at Sandringham, the Duke pointed at a tall, thin man with a beard and asked, loudly enough for the man to hear, *Is that a terrorist?* There was a sharp intake of breath all round, but fortunately the man in question took it well and just laughed. But what if he had been an immigrant Muslim, there with a group of militant friends, touchy about the assumption that all Muslims are terrorists. What then?

"I think there is little doubt that there are some people who will always remain insensitive to the reactions of others, and there will always be people who refuse to consider changing the way they communicate. They are not my target audience. I want to address those people who want to be effective communicators, who understand the need to consider how they are being received and understood, and who want to be sure they are getting it right.

At Norman's invitation, I outlined my own take on the remaining four essential elements.

WHERE ARE YOU HEADING?

I said, "The structure is vital. That's element number two. If your listeners start to wonder where you are heading, you risk losing them.

"Element number 3 is about the way you sound. It's your voice, your vocal variety, even your use of drama, and whether you sound prescriptive or encouraging. The fourth element is about ownership of the idea. That is one of the most significant tactics in the process of persuasion. People are always more prepared to do what they decide for themselves than to do what you tell them to do.

"And finally, element number five is about the follow-up. It's about Making It Happen, it's about feedback, it's about developing the relationship. All those things represented by the simple gesture of writing a short note.

"Someone asked me once if writing a follow-up note was only for business situations. What do you think? Suppose you met someone new in a social context and received a handwritten note from them the next day, saying how much they enjoyed meeting you. Would you consider that strange? Or would you be impressed and want to meet them again?"

Chapter 8 Summary

Getting Acceptance

Is the target audience business or lay?

Norman Sinclair says it's people. How they communicate will be the same even though the context may change. However, always concentrate on those who have a need for what you are offering, because the public is not your audience – it *contains* your audience.

He asked me to construct an imaginary scene of an 18th century courtier delivering a vital message to the king, to highlight five essential elements of communication:
- Preparation
- Structure
- Delivery and the way you sound
- Emotional connection
- Follow-up

When I won my first race at Blackheath Harriers, the Chairman didn't realise his remarks were a put down.

Think about the structure – where are you heading? How do you sound? And don't forget the follow-up, to develop the relationship.

THE MAN WHO GAVE AWAY HIS LOTTERY WIN

Nine

Does your wife snore?

Norman then told me a story – a true story – that made me realise something about myself. He said he was approached by a copywriter once who asked his advice about how to react to criticism of his writing. We all have to satisfy the demands of clients, and what they say about our work is often ill-informed and unfair. Creative people such as copywriters and designers can be very sensitive about their work, and this fellow would get upset and lose the will to live when he was asked to change something he had written.

I immediately empathised with the man he was talking about. I have always found it hard to take criticism, and when someone starts with, "If I may …" or "I'm not being personal, but …" or any other preamble to a hatchet job, I tend to bristle. It meant I was already onside with the chap in Norman's narrative. But I wanted to hear how he handled the approach.

"This chap," said Norman, "let's call him Bill, because that was his name, was an experienced copywriter. If not well stricken in years, his bloom of youth had long since faded. He worked in the Creative Department of a large direct marketing business. His work was passed to the relevant unit in the Marketing Department, where a Campaign Controller would collect the comments of all relevant people and feed them back to Bill. The Campaign Controllers were young graduates learning the Marketing business, and unfortunately they were not skilled in dealing with sensitive creatives like Bill.

"Some of the comments they fed back came from people less knowledgeable than Bill, people with limited experience of selling or persuasive writing. They would challenge some of Bill's grammar, they took issue with his use of the Oxford comma, they disputed the sequence of his arguments, they even questioned his practice of ending the page, for the turn, in the middle of a sentence instead of a full stop.

"Some of the comments were valid, others clearly not. But most of them caused steam to pour from Bill's ears. He took every criticism personally, and resented being corrected by people he considered less able, less well-educated, less experienced than himself. As a consequence, relations were strained between Bill and Marketing. He wanted my opinion. Correction, he wanted me to tell him he was right.

"Now, the reason I am telling you about Bill's problem is that we are talking about how to achieve effective communication, and that means taking account of problems. I think you would agree that when two people are at loggerheads, communication is difficult. When that happens regularly, something has to change. And that "something" is attitude. With a different attitude, and Bill's greater experience of life, he could have got a different outcome. I decided to ask him a question he did not expect.

AN UNEXPECTED QUESTION

"I asked him, *Does your wife snore?*"

"*What?*" he was so startled he didn't know how to react or respond. Then I could see that he was getting angry, but not with me.

"*Forgive me, I said, laughing. It's a serious question, but I had a reason for springing the question on you like that. Your reaction to the question is the relevant point. So is your reaction to your wife's snoring, if she does in fact snore. Let me explain.*

"*Consider the several parts of that question. First of all, it's impertinent. It's a personal question I have no right to ask. Why did I ask it, and why did I ask it in the way that I did? That's my contribution to the dialogue. I had a purpose, which was to provoke and observe your reaction. Secondly, there's*

*your reaction itself, and that's your contribution. You are
thinking: that's an odd question, or a personal one, I don't
think I like it, he's making me uncomfortable, it's causing me
to re-think how I feel about him. All those things. All
prompted by what? By the question itself, or because it was
asked by someone outside your family? We might notice and
react to all those kinds of elements in a conversation, even if
we don't respond to them. They colour our relationships.*

*"If your wife does snore, I continued, or has some other
irritating habit, I'd be interested to know if it makes you cross.
Or do you ignore it because your regard for her is greater than
the irritation she might cause. In any case, my question
prompted you to consider just how you do or would react to
your wife's snoring. Isn't that why you started to get angry.
Not because of my impertinence, but because of your built-up
irritation with her snoring."*

"Bill took in what I was saying and was quiet for a
while. Then he asked me how that was relevant to his
problem with the Campaign Controllers. I replied that
there was a direct connection. It all hinged on his
attitude. The things that other people say and do will
always have the potential to irritate us, mainly because
we believe that *it's not the way we would do those things.*
Isn't that why we don't like the way someone else drives
a car? They don't change gears when you would have
done, they brake too late or too early, and as for parallel
parking ... well, I'm sure you get my point.

"Bill said he thought I was trying to get him to change his personality, become more tolerant, more accepting, lower his standards. He said he was too old to change his personality and was unwilling to lower his standards. Now here's the important bit. I wasn't asking him to do either.

WHAT OUTCOME DO YOU WANT?

"I said there was another way, an approach that would appeal to his rational self. I asked him to consider the outcome he wanted. I said, let's start with your wife's snoring. Suppose you complain, how would that make her feel? Is that the outcome you want? Now think about your dealings with the Campaign Controllers. If you contest their feedback, you know there will be a row and some unpleasantness. Is that the outcome you want? Always think about the outcome you want and take the course of action that is most likely to get you there. It's that simple. And it's a lot easier to adopt that approach than you might imagine.

"Think about this, I added, suppose you are being interviewed for a new job and the interviewer mispronounces a word that you feel strongly about. Suppose he says conTROVersy instead of CONtroversy or caLYbre instead of CALibre or ceREEbral instead of CERebral. Would you correct him? Or would you consider it more important to avoid offending him? Your focus would be on the outcome you want, which is to be offered the job, so you would modify your behaviour accordingly. Wouldn't you?

"The lightbulb came on in his head. What had I done? I had merely prompted him to consider an alternative approach to disagreements, in a way that gave him a rational justification. Remember, when we speak about communication, we tend to think about the speaker, not the listener. But the listener plays a vital role in the conversation. At times we are the speakers, but a lot of the time we are the listeners. Are we good listeners? Bill may have thought he was a good listener, but chances are he was a critical, intolerant listener. As a copywriter, he was a communicator. Was he a good one? A good communicator needs to be a good listener as well. Do you think that would find a place in the messages you communicate?"

It was only a step away from that to start thinking about feedback. So I told Norman, "I agree with everything you have said about how we react to criticism, but isn't it part of the bigger issue of feedback? About how we deliver feedback and how we respond to it? Actually, you might say that criticism is a form of feedback."

LET'S TALK ABOUT FEEDBACK

He smiled and nodded in agreement, then suggested I tell him my thoughts on feedback.

"I think there are three kinds of feedback," I began, "or rather, three circumstances in which you get feedback. First, when you haven't asked for it, but others volunteer what they think of what you have done or said. Second, when you request it, in relation to something specific that you have done or said, and third, when it comes indirectly, when it is implicit in the behaviour of others. For example, if you deliver a great speech and get asked back, that's positive feedback. If people leave before you have finished, that's negative feedback. It's not stated explicitly, but you know exactly what is meant.

"Volunteered feedback can be either positive or negative. Frequently, it's a statement of how you made someone feel. If you are a performer, fans will say you did well. That's just a way of saying you made them feel good. Usually a fan would consider it presumptuous to detail the specifics of your performance, complimenting you, for example, on the clever way you segued from point A to point B.

"Requested feedback is quite different and needs to be carefully thought out. You need to be cautious about asking people randomly for feedback, because that can sound like a plea for compliments. I'd always recommend having a good reason for choosing the person whose feedback you want and make your request specific. Ask what they thought about certain particular things. Even if it's a general topic, such as how you come across in a meeting, unless the feedback is specific, you will not be able to do anything with it.

Feedback that merely says you were good may lift your spirits, but it will have little value beyond that. I'll come back to Requested Feedback in a moment. Let me first say something about Indirect Feedback.

"Performers are usually sensitive to Indirect Feedback. Speakers will look for little signs, such as nodding and smiling, during the speech, and that will tell them how well they are connecting with their listeners. I think we all do that in our day to day dealings and conversations. We read the body language of others, often without realising we are doing it, and modify our behaviour or what we are saying accordingly. In fact, body language is probably the most common form of feedback. I saw a speaker deliver a performance that may have been below par. He thought some people kept their distance afterwards (negative body language) so he took the initiative and approached them one by one, with his charm on main beam, overpowering any negative feelings they might have had and leaving them feeling positive towards him.

"Let me now go back to the Requested Feedback. There is a protocol that is honoured more in the breach, and that is about the way to respond. I believe there is an obligation to respect the feedback we have requested, even if we then do not act on it. Let's suppose you are going to deliver a speech and you ask an experienced speaker to evaluate your performance. Suppose your evaluator's feedback includes a reference to the lack of a cohesive structure, and you immediately defend yourself saying, *I didn't have the time to prepare properly, so I cobbled together a few ideas and just busked it.* Bad form. First of all, don't ask for feedback on some half-baked performance and secondly, understand that such a self-justification amounts to dismissing the evaluation. In effect you are saying the feedback is invalid because you hadn't properly prepared, and it does not apply to your usual standard of speaking. It's bad manners and may alienate a former ally.

THE VITAL TAG QUESTION

"Let me add something on the way we express our feedback. Have you ever come across the term, Tag Question? It's a way of modifying what could otherwise sound bossy or prescriptive. My wife's father had a way of creating resistance to his pronouncements because he could make a statement about the time of day sound prescriptive. If he said *It's getting dark* it sounded like he was telling everyone to fall in line behind him and agree it was getting dark. At first I couldn't understand why there was so much resistance within his family, but I soon realised that such an habitual conversational style can be wearisome.

"His wife had a different style. She'd say *It's getting dark, don't you think?* That's a Tag Question. It turns a statement into a question with a tag that invites your opinion. That simple device can make all the difference, especially when you are offering your opinion, don't you think? There is another device I would recommend. If you are suggesting some change in the other person's behaviour, instead of issuing a command, however well-intentioned, e.g. *Don't be so abrupt,* you might consider phrasing it as a question: *Have you considered trying a more roundabout way of expressing yourself?*

"You can even boost the impact of your praise, using certain conversational hypnotic phrases, the kind that are used in NLP. One that I have used myself is, *I wonder if you noticed how powerfully you affected your audience? You may never know how much they are going to change their behaviour, because of you.*"

The Tag Question was clearly a vital cog in the machinery of effective communication. It was time to break for lunch.

Chapter 9 Summary

Does your wife snore?

Norman tells the story of Copywriter Bill who had a problem with accepting criticism of his work by those he considered his intellectual inferiors. Bill's thinking was adjusted by being asked an unexpected question and considering his habitual response to other people's irritating behaviour.

The rationale he needed for appearing to lower his standards or expectations was the advice to consider the outcome of usual reaction – did he really want to provoke a row?

When it comes to receiving feedback, we must first be tolerant listeners. If we request feedback, we must respect the feedback we are given. On the other hand, when we give feedback, it is important not to sound prescriptive, and that's where the Tag Question comes in – a vital cog in the machinery of communication.

THE MAN WHO GAVE AWAY HIS LOTTERY WIN

Ten

Lunch break

Norman led me into the dining area adjoining his kitchen. He said there were two important purposes in the lunch interval. First, it was always good to have a break with a change of scene, especially if you are engaged in some creative activity, as you and I are, and second, to eat wholesome food. Lunch was hot carrot and coriander soup with brown bread, followed by an Asian salad of chopped Kale, Snow Peas, Red Pepper, Carrot and Avocado, with Thai basil and a Tamari-Ginger vinaigrette dressing. He told me it was both vegan and gluten free, showing me the original recipe, which included Edamame beans. I'd never heard of them before and mispronounced them to rhyme with game, but he corrected me, calling them edda-may-mee. Said they were just young soya beans, and should be avoided at all costs.

"I thought soya products were good substitutes for meat," I said, "have I got it wrong?"

"Lots of people have it wrong," was his reply. "Soya has some benefits but it contains oestrogen-like compounds called isoflavones. They are known to cause cancer. I couldn't find a definitive answer to the question about soya, so I decided not to take the risk. There are other sources of protein."

I asked him what had turned him vegetarian and he said, "Sausages. That's how it all began. I saw a film clip of sausages being made, and all the unappetising bits of the animal, such as lips and lids, that are churned into the mix. Then I read that all processed meats, such as sausages, are as bad for you as smoking. One report apparently claimed that the World Health Organisation was planning to ban them, saying they were among the most cancer-producing substances, alongside arsenic and asbestos.

WHAT TURNED HIM OFF 'DEAD FOOD'

"The award-winning nutritionist, Bonnie Taub-Dix, wrote *Read It Before You Eat It* and said she avoids sausages, bacon and hot dogs like the plague. People trust what she says, so I decided to do that as well. It was hard to give up sausages, because I used to love them. Really enjoyed them, along with bacon, in a full English breakfast, especially when I was staying in some hotel away from home. Then I met someone who had worked in a sausage factory and he never ate them again afterwards.

"I went to visit a friend whose father had a chicken farm. The sight of all those chickens crammed into cages, their beaks cut off and sitting in their own excrement, really turned me off. I began to take notice of films about man's cruelty to animals, often in the name of food farming, and I finally decided I had to quit eating meat. I'm not a campaigner on the subject. I'm quite happy for others to eat meat, but I carefully choose what I eat. Some years ago, I heard that a prominent speaker and author had been diagnosed with terminal cancer. He and his wife changed their diet. They went completely organic. He's still going strong, and the cancer has disappeared. That influenced my thinking.

"The clincher came when I saw a destitute man eating a can of dog food. I asked him why he was doing that and he said it was food. Passed by the Food Standards Agency, so it must be OK to eat. I read the labels on cans of dog food. *With beef* meant 3% beef and animal derivatives. Yes, derivatives, whatever that means. The rest was all kinds of rubbish. It told me that the food industry was selling stuff that was far removed from natural, healthy food. And what they put on their labels is questionable, especially to one who specialises in verbal communication! I don't go as far as Donald Trump, but I have learned not to trust what is claimed about food, processed food in particular, and I've heard many horror stories about the way food is handled in restaurant kitchens.

"I started eating 'living' food – vegetables, fruit, nuts and berries – and cut out dead food. Meat. Felt better almost immediately and lost some weight. That's not all I do. I run every day for half an hour. Some days I cover more ground than on other days, but I don't let that bother me. I am not training for a competition, just running for the exercise and the pleasure it gives me. In my younger days I used to run marathons, half marathons and cross country.

"The diet and the exercise are part of the new way of being that I embarked upon. I think I mentioned it when we first met, yesterday. And how is it connected to the communication programme? Very simply, the way you are, the way you live, will influence the way you communicate. When I gave up my job and went freelance, I gradually lost some of my interpersonal skills. Because I didn't have colleagues to interact with. As a result, I sometimes tried too hard in conversations and it gave rise to resistance.

TAKE TIME TO SMELL THE ROSES

"To correct this, I have built one vital element into my new way of life, and that is to spend some time each day just smelling the roses, speaking metaphorically. I spend that time either doing nothing, or pottering about in the garden, letting my mind wander, refreshing the spirit, so to speak. There's always a notebook nearby, because I like to make a note of any bright ideas that might arise.

This has enabled me to be more confident about my beliefs and it's freed me from the need to impress. When I'm with others now, I am often quite content just to listen. My stress level has dropped significantly.

"It's said that the man in the grey flannel suit, i.e. the typical businessman, will eventually acquire his badge of office – a peptic ulcer. And that will certainly impair his performance. I read recently that the Mental Health Foundation has reported that 1 in 6 people in the UK suffer from depression, and about the same proportion of managers admit to taking time off work due to stress.

"500 years ago, Henry VIII came to the throne of England as a lively, handsome, attractive man. Over the years he became increasingly ill-tempered and tyrannical, partly because he had leg ulcers, recorded as "sorre legge", and reacted viciously to those who commented adversely on it. Napoleon had stomach cancer, and that made him bad tempered as well. It put him at odds with his generals and that may have been why he ignored their advice at the Battle of Waterloo, and made some unusually poor decisions, which led to his defeat by Wellington. So you see, the pressures of life expose you to the risk of becoming unwell and behaving like a bear with a sore head. That's why I run and why I also take time to smell the roses.

"Did you know that sickness changes your social position? Sociologists regard sickness, especially long-term illness, as a form of social deviance. Yes, social deviance! Think back to your school days. If you were under the weather, you were excused gym and maybe even homework. These days, adults who have man flu, or even the real thing, expect to be regarded as invalids, and they excuse themselves from their social responsibilities.

THE 'IMPAIRED ROLE'

"There is even an official term for that state; it's called the Sick Role. But there is another more accurate name for an unwell person, and it's the Impaired Role. Here's the difference. The Sick Role describes your status as a person who is ill and cannot function normally, but who is expected to recover and resume previous activities. It's a short-term state. On the other hand, the Impaired Role describes a person whose reduced effectiveness is long-term or permanent. Most of the time, a sick person expects to recover soon and takes some sort of remedial action. Medicine, rest, doctor's advice, that sort of thing.

"The scary thing is that large numbers of people remain below par all the time. They are in the Impaired Role and either do not realise it or they are afraid to get the diagnosis for fear of losing their job. Men are more likely than women to conceal their impaired state, possibly because of the macho thing, the belief that it's unmanly to admit an illness or a weakness.. Does it get worse? Probably. The impairment would be due to some chronic disease, either physical or mental, and diseases do tend to get worse. So they are always performing less well than they could and possibly doing themselves harm by not getting the problem sorted. For 20 years I suffered from muscular pain, but since I resumed my regular stress-free running, the pain has gone.

"There is a connection between what I've been saying just now and the verbal communication we were discussing earlier. It's this: communication starts in the mind. If you allow your body to become less effective, less efficient, it will affect your mood, the way you think, your attitude to those you connect with."

As a club runner myself I was interested in his running regimen, especially his previous marathon experience, and asked how it came about. He said he would tell me about it, and how he learned a lesson about communication along the way, when we resumed our conversation inside the house. We walked around his garden for ten minutes before returning to the conservatory. My mind felt as clear as it had ever been.

Chapter 10 Summary

Lunch break

Norman explained that it was always important to take a break during creative activity, and to eat wholesome food. He had prepared a vegan meal and explained what had turned him off meat. His health had improved since he gave up meat and started eating only 'living food'. He mentioned seeing a destitute man eating a can of pet food, in the belief that it was healthy food.

He said he had added a new element to his life – taking time to smell the roses. He quoted the Mental Health Foundation's report that 1 in 6 people in the UK suffered from depression, and the same proportion of managers take time off because of stress.

King Henry VIII and Napoleon carried illnesses that affected their behaviour and possibly their judgement too. Norman drew the distinction between the Sick Role and the Impaired Role, which can have a bearing on the way we communicate.

Eleven

Getting it right personally

When we resumed after lunch, Norman opened with, "If we are going to consider the effect of what we say, I'd like us to think about interpersonal communication, the stuff that goes on between partners and friends. Business communication may be different from what goes on at home and among friends, but the fundamentals are the same. I know a relationship counsellor who understands the process very well and is incredibly helpful to couples whose relationships are on the rocks, but she learned the hard way. Her own relationship broke up because of poor communication with her partner. It wasn't all her fault, but she didn't understand what was going on with him, and she reacted badly. And now it's too late.

"A close parallel would be the process of bargaining in a market east of Istanbul. Have you ever had the experience of haggling for a watch or a garment?"

I said I had, and with some success. I said I'd been in Dubai with a female colleague who wanted to buy a particular robe. We approached several stalls and established the general price for that robe. We then went to another stall where I went through the charade of haggling over the price of some garment I had no intention of buying. When we reached the point at which he would budge no further, I waved my hand dismissively to signify I was no longer interested and walked away. He called me back. "How much you pay?" he asked.

I shook my head and pointed at the robe we wanted to buy, as though it were a cheaper alternative. He quoted me the same price as everyone else. I offered him half and he looked affronted. Then I said I would pay his price, but I wanted two. As he picked up two of the same size, I shook my head and said I wanted one of a smaller size (for my own wife, who was slimmer than my colleague). The stallholder grinned and slapped me on the shoulder, saying, "TWO wife!" I got the deal I wanted, two robes for the price of one.

Norman laughed, and said, "You obviously understand the process, but let's spell it out. Many westerners can't understand why those stallholders don't just state a price and stick to it. They fail to understand that the sale is only a part of the process. The market people quote an inflated price, expecting you to resist. If you pay, they win. They get a higher price. If you bargain, they enjoy the development of the relationship. They enjoy reading your manner to see how far you will go, just like a game of poker. They relish the little tussle and they usually end up winning, even if it is only to make a sale at their bottom price. By giving in to you they place you under an obligation to buy. One important element is the saving of face – neither party must be embarrassed – another is the enjoyment of the dialogue. When you allowed him to think he was sharing your secret of having two wives, that made his day.

TOUJOURS LA POLITESSE

"The American linguist, Robin Lakoff, offers three rules for politeness, and they apply in the situation you described:

1. Don't impose – keep your distance
2. Give options – allow the other to have a say
3. Be friendly – maintain camaraderie

"What you did, in the Dubai bargain, satisfied all three rules. By walking away from the first deal you were respecting his line in the sand. That was rule number one. By asking for two for the price of one, you gave him a better option than the half price alternative. Finally, the implicit joke about two wives gave him something to laugh about and slap you on the shoulder like an old friend.

"Now consider meeting someone of the opposite sex for the first time. Sometimes everything clicks into place.

You laugh at the same things, you find the same rhythm, you might even finish each other's sentences, and you feel a surge of pleasure at meeting that person. Another time you meet someone whose rhythm is all wrong. You speak over each other, there are long silences, no feeling of togetherness. Much of this is instinctive, but it need not be permanent. There are times when the first meeting is a disaster, but a good relationship develops later.

LEARNING FROM PORCUPINES

"The philosopher Schopenhauer illustrates this with the example of porcupines. In a cold winter they will snuggle up to one another for shared warmth. But they accidentally spike each other and have to withdraw, and that makes them cold. So they have to make a number of adjustments until they can be warm without getting hurt. That's how it could be in developing relationships. But remember, how we communicate can make all the difference between success and failure.

"For example, we all have our own communication patterns and we can assume that others have the same. It can cause us to misread the signals. If the other person behaves as we would behave when angry with someone, we will tend to assume that they are angry with us. We will then respond to that imagined anger as though it were real, and so on, making a mountain out of nothing at all. So, what's the answer? Simply ask the other person what's wrong. Let me give you an example.

"Peter resigned as the chorus manager of a singing group. At the next rehearsal, the chorus director, Susan, was greeting members with her usual hug, but she missed out Peter, just waving to him across the room. Guess what he thought? That she was angry with him. It caused him to be very withdrawn throughout the rehearsal but when it was over, he went over and said, *Are you cross with me?* Nothing had been further from her mind, so she was startled, and they were able to resolve the matter very quickly and she said (and isn't it significant?), she said, *Can I have a hug now?* She had thought Peter had denied *her* a hug at the start of the meeting!"

I thought about that for a moment, and asked him, "But wasn't it understandable that Peter should feel that Sue was angry with him? After all, he had just dropped out of a senior role on the committee, and perhaps there was a back story behind that?"

"Quite right," said Norman. "There often is a back story. The man whose snoring wife had built up a reservoir of irritation and that caused him to be intolerant of anything that irritated him. Let's see what we can learn about personal relationships from this. When two people decide to get together, either in marriage or some other form of committed relationship, isn't it fair to assume that they start with a high regard for each other? More than that, they have respect as well as a liking for each other.

SAFEGUARDING THE RELATIONSHIP

"It is possible, but not inevitable, that they will always have that same high regard for each other. Is there something they do to safeguard that relationship and prevent it from going off the rails? Yes, there is. Any relationship is complex, but there is one thing they can put in place at the start, and keep following, to avoid a major split. And that is the right pattern of communication. Here are the rules:

1. Always tell the truth
2. If in doubt, ask for the explanation
3. Treat the other as the No.1 person around
4. Be responsible for their emotional and physical safety

"All four rules are about the way you communicate. Rules 1 and 2 are obviously about verbal communication, but 3 and 4 are about your attitude and the non-verbal behaviour that stems from it. If your partner irritates you, let it go, because to react will be to diminish them. If your partner is unhappy, consider it your fault for not protecting them or providing the necessary reassurance. You should build these rules into your personal DNA, and you will never humiliate, fight with or grow apart from the most important person in your life."

I asked if he thought such an ideal was achievable. His reply surprised me.

"These are not techniques, like learning how to speak in public. These are guidelines for one's behaviour in general. When a man shouts at his wife, I would ask him if he would speak like that to his Managing Director. And yet, his wife is far more important than his Managing Director. And when a wife speaks sarcastically to her husband, she diminishes him and takes away his self-respect. It's all about attitude, and that is a vital ingredient of interpersonal communication."

I said it sounded like a case for equal treatment, and that was not yet in the culture of every nation. What was the key to connecting across cultures?

THE KEY WORD, 'RESPECT'

"One word," he replied. "Respect. You cannot master a range of behaviours to cover all cultures, but the single most important ingredient of successful communication across cultures is Respect. You don't need instruction to realise that interrupting a person when they are speaking is rude, or invading their personal space bubble is disrespectful. Of course, different nations have different ways of communicating, and they can be irritating if they differ too much from our own. For example, the American-led Western way is very direct, whereas Arabs and Orientals can be very roundabout. Each can find the other tiresome. Who should make the adjustment?

"That depends on which side of the table you are sitting. In every relationship and every transaction, there tends to be two roles – dominant and supplicant. The dominant person has the power, the supplicant is the one with the need. There's a well-known story of a Big Shot who wanted more butter, while in a restaurant. He asked the busy (and harassed) waiter several times. Finally, losing patience, the said, *Do you know who I am?* The waiter paused long enough to say, *No idea, but do you know who I am? I'm the one with the butter, and you're not getting any!*

"In his book, *Culture, Language and Personality*, Edward Sapir says, *No two languages are ever sufficiently similar to be considered as representing the same social reality. The worlds in which different societies live are distinct, not merely the same world with different labels attached.* I think that means each country's language expresses its attitudes and values, not just descriptions of the events and objects around. The best way to avoid a tangle of misunderstanding is to act out of respect.

"Dr Deborah Tanner, the American Professor of Linguistics, says that each person's life is lived as a series of conversations. She also says that the conversational style makes or breaks relationships. I think she is right,

114

and that is why I am having this conversation with you. If you agree with what I am saying and incorporate this thinking into your professional speeches, you can make a positive contribution to improving people's approach to interpersonal relationships."

HOW WE SIGNAL OUR INTENT

I asked Norman which element of verbal communication best communicates our intent, and he quickly said, "Tone of voice."

He explained that many problems in relationships arise out of taking offence at something that was said. "When someone takes offence," he went on, "I always tell them that the offence lies in the intention, and the intention is usually conveyed, not in what was said, but in the way that it was said. And that is why we need to pay attention to our tone of voice. I think that is fairly obvious, but what is less well understood is how to defuse such a misunderstanding.

"Imagine you've said something that has plainly upset the other person. Or suppose you have something on your mind, you are concentrating on something that is causing you to feel irritated. Your wife asks you a question that breaks your concentration. You reply brusquely. The tone of your response derives from the subject your mind was on. That's where it belongs, yet it

115

is she who receives your irritation. How do you put it right?

"Analysing or re-stating what you said could only make things worse, so simply say something completely different, in a friendly tone of voice that signals all is well between you."

I had never thought of that. Good advice.

Chapter 11 Summary

Getting it right personally

We talked about the process and meaning of haggling in an Eastern market, and how westerners often fail to understand the mindset behind the haggling process. It's how the shopkeeper engages with the customer and, by accepting the latter's lower price, imposes an obligation to buy. An essential part of the transaction is always to allow the other to save face. This is implicitly endorsed by the American linguist, Robin Lakoff, who offers three rules for politeness.

Talking about the way we start relationships, Norman mentioned Schopenhauer's example of how porcupines keep warm together, and offered four rules for safeguarding a relationship. The key word, which is the lynchpin of cross-cultural communication, is Respect, especially as, according to Edward Sapir, *No two languages are ever sufficiently similar to be considered as representing the same social reality*.

The one element that best communicates our intent in verbal communication is tone of voice.

THE MAN WHO GAVE AWAY HIS LOTTERY WIN

Twelve

What's the story?

Respect, tone of voice and politesse. They are all linked, but I needed a moment to take them in, to internalise the effect of the realisation that we – that is to say I – will usually assume that the listener will have the same cultural background, make the same assumptions, respond in the same way to metaphor, humour, irony and even, on occasion, to well-intentioned rudeness. It reminded me of some occasions when an offhand joking remark delivered with a straight face had been mistaken for arrogance. I'd have to tread with greater care in future.

In the pause, Norman told me about a man who travelled the world teaching people, mainly business people, to tell stories in their presentations. Storytelling, according to that man, Doug Stevenson, is an essential leadership skill, one that will enable you to be persuasive and influential. It will set you apart from others, it will make your ideas memorable.

"Doug once told me," said Norman, "that he was giving a talk or a seminar, and those in the audience were busily scribbling notes, and then he said something that caused an interesting reaction. He spoke six words and everyone stopped writing and sat forward in their seats, to listen more attentively. He noticed that and, at his next seminar, he said those same six words, and got the same reaction.

ONCE UPON A TIME

"Those six words were, *Let me tell you a story.* Now the question is, why did that happen? The answer is, Conditioning. Most of us were told stories in our childhood. Stories that began, *Once upon a time* and usually ended *happily ever after.* Children love stories, and often want to hear the same stories over and over again, in the same way. They will even correct you if you diverge from the usual version.

"What is about stories, and what is their relevance to what you and I are talking about? What is the role of stories in communication? Are they simply a distraction from the message? Absolutely not! They enhance the message. But only if they are told in the right way. Especially if they are acted out.

"Here's how it works. When you tell a story, you provide context and the characters in your narrative. In effect you create a stage play and invite your listeners to occupy the front seats. Now what's the most important element of a stage play? Dialogue. So your story has to be full of dialogue. Next, who are the characters? What are their names? How are they connected to one another and to the point of the story? What do they look like and how do they behave?

"Remember *Snow White and the seven …*"

"Dwarfs."

"… *Vertically challenged mine workers,*" he concluded with a laugh. Of course, I immediately remembered the excellent Disney cartoon film that brought to life the familiar old story and made it so memorable. I remembered the colours, the characters, their antics and the tale by the Brothers Grimm of a young girl's exile into a dangerous forest by her wicked stepmother. I remember being cheered by the kindness of the little miners who took her into their household.

"But can you remember the moral of the story?" asked Norman.

"Oh yes," said I, "it was the eventual triumph of good over evil. I remember how Snow White perished at the hands of her wicked stepmother, but was rescued by the good prince. So, good will triumph when well-intentioned people get together and support each other. Something like that."

"Not bad," said Norman. "The film was first shown in 1937, and re-released many times since then. The story is simple, it's fanciful, and the moral is quite straightforward, but the cartoon film is one of the most memorable films of all time. And why? For the same reason that people stop to listen when you say, *Let me tell you a story.*

NEURAL COUPLING

"In fact, there is science to back this up. Recent research has discovered that stories activate more of the listener's brain than facts alone. Not only that, the listener's brain fires in the same pattern as the speaker's brain. They call this *neural coupling*. What it means is that a story will synchronise the brains of the speaker and the listener.

"One consequence is that the listener becomes emotionally engaged through the story. Psychologists call this *narrative transport*. And what does that produce? One of the most powerful elements of persuasive communication. It creates *empathy* with the speaker.

"All this was discovered by scanning the brains of the speaker and listener at the same time, using something called FMRI – Functional Magnetic Resonance Imaging. The process measures brain activity by detecting blood flow. When an area of the brain is activated, there is an increased flow of blood to that area. Now, when the brain is presented with factual information, only two of its regions are activated. Those are the areas that process language. Storytelling makes more areas light up. And the same areas light up in the brains of the speaker and the listener.

"It gets better. In any significant communication, the first requirement is to get and hold the attention of your listeners. The tension in a well-prepared story will achieve that for you. Just think of an action movie that makes you hold your breath when the hero is approaching some hidden danger. You remain riveted.

"Uri Hasson at Princeton says that a good story not only synchronises the brain of your listener with your own, but because it has activated the same parts of the listeners' brains as your own, those listeners can come to believe that the story belonged to them, that it was an event they themselves had experienced. While they were listening to your story, they were subconsciously searching their own brains for their own life experiences that had produced the same emotions as the ones you evoked during your story.

"Now that's a lot of science to take in. But here's a quick summary. Use stories to deliver or illustrate your message. Keep them simple, but always tell them like a mini movie. Create images and scenes that the listener can visualise, and include an element of tension to grab and hold the attention. Avoid clichés because they carry no meaning and get in the way of the story. Use the story to connect with the emotions of your listeners and you can create empathy. That's what will make them ready to accept your message or your proposition."

Norman paused again, and drank a glass of water. Much as I enjoyed what he had told me about the value of storytelling, I was glad of the break. He asked me if I had a story I could tell him, along the lines of what he had just told me. I had a story ready about getting picked for the team.

WHAT I LEARNED FROM CHARLIE

This was my story:

When Charlie was eight years old, his classmates decided on an impromptu game of football. They all lined up and the 2 captains took turns in choosing their teams. Charlie was tubby with a round sallow face and spiky black hair. He wore a shapeless white T-shirt and had fat legs with baggy shorts that came down to his knees. He knew he was not athletic and was afraid he would not get picked. Does that sound familiar? Remember the time you stood in a line, waiting to be picked, afraid to make eye contact in case you were rejected?

Every time someone else was picked, and the line grew shorter, Charlie became increasingly anxious. He hung his head. As he feared, he was picked only when there was no one else left. The captain of his team simply

124

beckoned, as though there was no need to even call out his name. I'm sure you know how Charlie felt. Remember when that happened to you, or to someone you knew?

The match started, and Charlie stood about, trying not to get in the way. But eventually the ball reached him and he started to run with it at his feet. But his shorts were loose and they fell around his ankles, tripping him up, and he fell on the ball. Everyone burst out laughing and the game stopped while he picked himself up and hitched up his shorts with a big grin on his face. That surprised everyone.

Charlie learned a valuable lesson that day. He learned that he could make people laugh.

Getting picked is one of the biggest challenges most of us face – for a job, for a business contract, for a relationship. You have to do something extra, something different, something that makes you stand out from the rest. Like Charlie's unexpected grin. Something that makes people want to pick you.

Norman applauded gently. "It was a vivid story, and I could just see Charlie standing there, looking embarrassed and feeling wretched. It's a familiar experience, and you told it conversationally. I connected with you and with Charlie. And it's the kind of story we can all tell in a business context or among the people we know. Now you could have told it even more dramatically. You could have stood up and acted out the whole scene. That would have made it even more memorable.

"Think back to your frock-coated messenger. He has an important message to deliver to the king. If he simply states the message, he may not get the full attention of the king, and he will fail to get the action he wants the king to take. If he tells a story about the circumstances that gave rise to the message, the king can get the point and decide he needs to release additional resources to solve the problem. Now let me tell you a story about the impact of praise.

THE IMPACT OF PRAISE

"Sally was just 23 in the Far East when her marriage broke up. Leaving her three young children behind, she went to India. One day a telegram arrived. It was from her school friend Helen, and just said, *Baby dead*. She hurried back and Helen told her, *Your kids were being neglected and baby Girlie died of starvation. Go see your sons. They are in a bad way too.*

"With the help of the commander of the local US military base, Sally kidnapped her sons and the Americans flew them in a bomber to India, where Sally placed them in a boarding school. The younger boy was 3 and a half. His brother was a year older. They couldn't speak a word of English.

"The brothers grew up at boarding school with hardly any parenting, but they did well. Then one day, something quite extraordinary happened. Something that changed the outlook of the younger brother, when he was 15 years old. He was approached by the English lecturer at the university who said, *Give me your opinion on this English paper. Has he got it right on irony?* The lecturer was asking the opinion of a 15-year old schoolboy! He said that boy was the best writer of English that he had come across.

"It was the greatest praise the boy had ever had! Can you imagine how he felt? At last he gained a sense of his self-worth from someone else. He went on to author 8 books about excellence in verbal communication. This was the boy who might have starved to death or grown up as an illiterate in the Far East. Just think of the change you can make to a person's life with a single act of praise!

"As you may have guessed, I was that boy, and Sally was my mother.

"Now you know something more about me. The story itself needs no embellishment because it is dramatic enough. But if you remember, I said I wanted to cover the essential elements in how we communicate with one another. The first was the effect of what we say on the listener. That's where stories come in. When I told you my own back story just now, it was not for the sake of the drama, but to create in you an understanding of my origins. With a bit of luck, that will have a helpful bearing on the rest of what we will be talking about today."

Chapter 12 Summary

What's the story?

Norman told me about Doug Stevenson, a professional speaker who travels the world telling speakers to tell stories in their speeches. Present them as mini stage plays full of dialogue, to bring the story to life and enable your listeners to re-create your message by remembering the story. He gave the example of Snow White and the seven 'vertically challenged mineworkers', and the magnificent cartoon film version produced by Walt Disney.

I told him my own story of Charlie, the awkward fat boy from whose example I learned a valuable lesson. Norman reminded me of the 18th century courtier we had conjured up earlier, and how that vivid image enabled me to remember five essentials of communication. He surprised me with his explanation of neural coupling, which explains why story-telling is so powerful in connecting with an audience.

Finally, Norman shared his own dramatic story and the impact of praise when he was a teenager.

Thirteen

Meeting expectations

"We all tell stories. They add colour and pictures to the conversation or the presentation, if it's a business situation. They make a significant contribution to the process of engaging the listener. When you impart factual information, your listener's attention may wander in and out. A story, on the other hand, can keep the listener engaged from start to finish. That's an important part of the effect you create on your listener.

"You might lead into your story with a prop, or a factoid, which is a false statement that many accept as true, and use your story as an example of what you mean. A common factoid is the claim, falsely attributed to Albert Mehrabian, that words contribute only 7% of the meaning.

"Remember, at this moment I am not talking about techniques for making speeches or presentations. I am talking about understanding the communication process, both in day-to-day conversations and in business presentations or speeches. The format is less important than the principles involved. If you understand the process of communication, you have a better chance of getting it right.

"In conversations, we all want to hear something we agree with before we hear something new or different. Consider controversial topics like Brexit or Abortion in Ireland. They are the kind of topics that can cause a rift. So how should they be handled? If you are the person with an opinion to express, you need to ease into the topic, first saying something general that establishes common ground. Then you have to use what I call a transition, which is a change of gear to move into your own point of view, but expressed in a way that allows for a different opinion.

DON'T PICK A FIGHT

"When you are with people you know, you may suppose they have similar views to your own, but If you just plunge into expressing your opinion, especially on a sensitive issue, you might quickly have a fight on your hands. People whose opinions differ from yours are more likely to give you air time if you show respect for the opposite point of view. Instead of saying *This is what I think,* you might begin by saying something like, *I've been trying to decide what to think about (subject). What do you think about (your point of view)?* That way you haven't declared your position, and you have invited the other person to declare theirs. You can then discuss the topic from both sides without picking a fight

"Business presentations and speeches are different. They have their own rules and criteria. Picture an audience waiting to hear you speak. What is in their minds? What would be a typical set of expectations? I was with a group of professional speakers, not long ago, and I asked them the question: *What are the expectations of your listeners as they sit waiting to hear you speak?*

"Most of them said, *Something new or unexpected, something they can use. Or they want to be entertained.* What that told me was that they had never given the matter serious thought. They had probably never even analysed their own expectations when they were listeners rather than speakers. I found that quite extraordinary. As a speaker, surely you must meet the expectations of your listeners. How can you do that if you don't know what they are? And if you don't give that some thought, it tells me what kind of speaker you are – someone who believes that communication is about transmission, a speaker who says, *I have things to say, and here they are.*

"Let's think about the expectations of your listeners, especially when you are making a business presentation. There are four I'd like to mention. But first, let me ask you to think about what happens in the minds and hearts of your listeners as you lead then through your message.

HOW DO YOU MAKE THEM FEEL?

"I know a professional speaker who starts by asking his audience their opinion about some "fact", something as simple as the greatest weight a man can carry. That's just a random example, not one that he actually uses. When they have made a commitment to their answer, he surprises them with the real answer, and uses their astonished response to prove that we all have uninformed beliefs. He asked my opinion. I said it was a clever way of making them receptive to his argument, but wondered if he had overlooked one vital ingredient in the mix.

"I said, *Have you considered their state of mind when you expose their ignorance? I mean, how would you feel if someone proved that you were wrong about some long-held belief – in public? Wouldn't you feel vulnerable, and perhaps a little stupid? Yes, when you remove that mistaken belief you create a hole that you can fill with your own answer. But isn't that an appeal to their heads? It's a factual correction. How do you cope with the feeling of vulnerability? There might even be a bit of resentment that you seem to know more than they do. How do you help them to recover their previous self-assurance?*

"He said that had never occurred to him before. More importantly, it helped him to understand what I meant about the expectations of an audience – to understand

134

not only what they want to hear, but also how they want you to make them feel. But let me go back to what I was saying about the four kinds of expectations people have when they attend a speaking event.

"First, it's my opinion that people who attend a speech or lecture are expecting to hear a confirmation of what they already know. Wouldn't that be your own first expectation? And why? Because it reassures you that you know something about the subject, and secondly it gives you confidence in the speaker. You'd give a metaphorical nod of agreement: *Yep, we are on the same page.* So what does that mean? It means there is no need to startle your listeners with a barrage of new facts or something controversial that might cause an argument. It's OK to establish common ground with known facts.

SHARED KNOWLEDGE

"There are two kinds of shared knowledge.
- The first is the kind I've just mentioned, the kind that gets the head nodding.
- The second is the unexpected reminder of things they have known but perhaps forgotten.

A man I know once said to me, after a presentation on public speaking, *Just imagine! I had to be reminded to focus on the needs of the audience! I've always known that, but my own speeches have gradually shifted towards displaying my*

135

own knowledge. I can think of three more common expectations.

"The second expectation is about the speaker's appearance, voice and manner. Those are the basic elements of a platform performer. Listeners want to be impressed. A speaker who turns up in T-shirt and jeans is making a statement that says, *This is how I like to be, and I don't care how you feel about it.* Question: Is that how they would dress for a job interview?
Is that how they would dress to make a new business presentation to a major client? That may not be the best way to create engagement.

Now think about the way you sound: a weak or grating voice can get in the way. It can kill respect. Think about broadcasters. Are there some newsreaders or weather forecasters whose voices you dislike? The voice should carry authority, and that can be developed. Not everyone is born with a commanding voice or presence.

"Of course, there are exceptions. People may point to billionaire entrepreneurs who make presentations in casual gear and get away with it. People like Steve Jobs could do that because they had made their millions and they didn't need to care about the impression they made. The average person, on the other hand, does need to care. When you have a message to deliver, and you want to persuade people to accept it, you need to care about the impression you make. If you are making a presentation, you will be judged even before you say a word. It therefore makes sense to dress well and look like a person of value. If you look as though you don't care about the opinions of your listeners, guess how they may react to your presentation?

"The third expectation in the minds of your listeners is entertainment. They want to enjoy the experience of listening to you. In a business presentation, that's easy to understand. Make them laugh, or make them feel good in some way. A business presentation is expected to be enjoyable. In a social conversation, there is a similar expectation, just on a different level. If someone is boring, or if someone is always talking about problems, I bet your heart would sink. You'd switch off. Or you'd end the conversation. That's not to say you should never share bad news. Just don't make a habit of it. Don't turn your conversation companions into your priest or counsellor!

TELL ME SOMETHING NEW

"The fourth expectation is for something new. People say, *Tell me something I didn't already know. Or give me a new angle on something I did know.* If they get nothing new they will feel they have wasted their time. I read a comment on FaceBook from a chap who attended a conference and was asked by the organiser for feedback. His reply said, *I'm not sure you would really want my feedback. Speaker A and Speaker B had useful content. The rest made me feel the whole occasion was a waste of time. It was just a rehash of stale old stuff.*

"People's expectations can be quite challenging. Perhaps even unfair. But if you want to persuade them to adopt your point of view – and that is the task of the teacher – you need to understand the process of persuasion. Let me give you an example.

"Suppose you want people to do something or buy something. The first step is to create engagement. Get their attention. Ask them a question about your proposition. Then start talking about the benefit they will get from listening to your proposition. Talk about the outcome they are likely to want, and tell them how to go about getting it. And then make it easy for them to take the action that will get them the outcome they want. In very simple terms, that's the sequence.

"Both in business presentations and in conversation, we want our listeners to accept our point of view. Sometimes that is our specific objective. So what we say is a sales pitch. As a sales pitch it has to follow the rules of selling. The first rule of selling, the strategy that never fails, is simply this: find out what the other person wants and offer it. And how do you find out what they want? You ask questions.

"And the next step? You've got to be a good listener."

Chapter 13 Summary

Meeting expectations

A story will keep your listeners engaged. It's part of the effect you have on them.

Be careful to avoid creating a rift, especially when discussing a controversial topic. Remember also the effect you can have on how your listeners feel, when you replace their long-held beliefs with your own ideas.

We are talking about understanding the process of communication, about creating and managing the expectations of the audience. There are four such expectations:

1. Confirmation of shared knowledge
2. Look and sound impressive
3. Entertainment
4. Something new

Start by engaging with the audience, using a prop, a factoid, something to establish common ground. Then consciously set about meeting their expectations.

Follow the rules of persuasion. Whether you are delivering a speech, a presentation, or just expressing your point of view in a conversation, you want your listeners to agree with you, so follow the rules of selling. And be a good listener.

Fourteen

Listening

Norman suddenly went silent and stared at me for perhaps ten seconds, long enough for a stricken boxer to get off the floor and resume fighting. Naturally, it felt a lot longer. I said nothing, because by then I had come to recognise that he did everything with a purpose. Finally he smiled and asked, "What do you suppose is the most underrated skill in verbal communication? It's listening.

"That's paradoxical. Surely it would be something you say, or some clever way of saying it? Not at all. It's simply being silent and paying attention. There is a significant difference between 'listening' and 'hearing'. The first involves the effort to understand and retain what is being said, to link it to what was said before and what is said next. Almost no one listens to everything that is being said to them, even in a one-to-one conversation.

"In the same way as we have expectations when we are in the audience of a speaker or presenter, those expectations define how we listen. We listen for information, to learn, for enjoyment, and to understand. We listen out of respect, and to make sense of what is happening around us. We listen when we are frightened, and when we have something to say. We listen for clues that tell us how we are doing.

"Can we taught to listen better? Why not? It's a skill and surely any skill can be taught. I've heard it said that the average person hears between 20,000 and 30,000 words a day. About half the time spent in communication is devoted to listening, and most of what we learn in our lifetime is through listening. And yet there are hardly any training courses on listening.

"We are all poor listeners. And why? Because we are easily distracted, and because we are bombarded daily by messages from many different sources – radio, TV, colleagues at work, our families – so that we respond selectively and forget most of what we hear.

RAPID REPEATING

"Good listeners in an audience actively signal that they understand what has been said, and that they agree. They smile, they nod, they sit forward in their seats. To get the most from listening, according to Peter Thomson, the UK's most prolific creator of information products, you could try what he calls *Rapid Repeating*. The way it works is for you, the listener, to repeat in your head the very words you have just heard. In a sense you become the echo of the speaker. If you do that, not only will you hear and remember more, you will look totally focused on the speaker."

"I tried that just now, as you were speaking," I said, "and it was not easy. But you are right. It does focus the mind."

"That's only one part of the process," said Norman. "What really goes on while we are listening is decoding. We notice verbal patterns that help us to understand, we hear things we agree with and some that we disagree with. We pick up what is safe to disagree with, and we are encouraged to nod or grunt when we agree.

"If we are being informed or instructed, telling is not enough. When I was at school, I wanted to do Latin. The others in my class had done Latin for four years previously. In the vac I had a tutor who raced through the subject, trying to bring me up to speed in three months. Each time he explained something, he asked if I understood, and I said yes. He looked surprised but went on.

"When I joined the Latin class at school, I wasn't able to keep up because, while I had understood what the tutor had taught me, I hadn't learned it well enough. A person can understand the instruction but not learn it. That

143

means you have to use a particular way of describing a new concept if you want your listener to take it on board and act on it. Ideally you should also verify that it has been correctly taken in. Don't expect that to be more than 50% of what was said.

"If you don't verify, they will simply return to their original way of doing things. And that is one of the main reasons why so many business presentations fail. They state a case but do not educate the listener. It's never enough to tell people things and expect them to remember. You need to change their thinking. Because if they think differently, they will act differently. And what is the key to that process? Think about the way they listen. Fit in with the way they understand, and answer their questions.

HOW PEOPLE LISTEN

"Let me just add a word about remembering what you have heard. Many people have a technique for remembering, often by association with something familiar. And when they need to recall something they go through the process of discovery. They work it out. That's not the same as learning and knowing. For example, you learned that 2 plus 2 is 4. No need to work it out. You just know the answer. But if you needed to list the first 10 US Presidents, you may have to go through a memory routine. Learning and knowing is not the same as learning and recalling.

144

"Now here's a bit of science. This is how people listen, especially during one of your business presentations. Most people can think or hear at 500 words per minute. When you are presenting, you might be speaking at about 150 words a minute. You are on Track 150, trying to take them from where they are to where you want them to be. But the brains of your listeners will have a surplus capacity of 350 words per minute – more than double the amount required to keep up with you. That surplus capacity, let's call it Track 350, will not remain dormant.

"Track 350 is where they deal with random thoughts that might intrude. That's also where they will process anything you say if they don't agree or don't understand. It is also where they will get their Aha! moments. So they will be dipping in and out of your Track 150, and they will miss bits of what you say. You need to recognise that this in-out, in-out will be taking place and help your listeners catch up by looping back, by reminding them of where you have been and where you are going next. This Track 350 idea is one of the crucial elements in business presentations, and it is usually overlooked.

"One more thing. Pay close attention to the way you are affected by the person or persons you are addressing. Don't you sometimes find you instinctively alter your speaking style and vocabulary, and even your accent, according to those you are addressing? I'm not sure why

145

that happens, but I just know it does. And it's important when it does. Because that means you are trying to find the right way to connect with the other person's level of understanding. That's why it's important."

FOLLOWING WHAT'S BEING SAID

I immediately understood what Norman was saying. In my Toastmasters club there were a number of members from Spain and other countries, and I sometimes struggled to get my point across to them. Even without trying I knew that certain linguistic jokes would go right over their heads. But beyond that, there were certain abstract concepts that I would find difficult to explain, but that may be because many of them are IT people, and they would more easily cope with factual content.

On the flip side, I often found it hard to understand them because of their thick foreign accents. In one-to-one conversations with them I would ask them to speak slowly, so that I could process and make sense of one piece of information at a time by concentrating really hard. And that taught me something else about the way we listen. We make sense of what is being said, and if we get it, we may switch off temporarily and ignore the words being spoken until the next step in the narrative that we need to understand. That's when we pay attention again.

I think most people do that in-and-out trick, but sometimes a person may simply make the appropriate sounds and signals to indicate that they are listening, without actually taking in what is being said. Norman had said as much when he told me that almost no one listens to everything that is being said to them.

I shared those thoughts with Norman, and he nodded in agreement, paused as though a different thought had occurred to him, and asked me an apparently oblique question. "You know how you assume that the other person is on the same wavelength as yourself, but when you ask them a simple question, their answer tells you they are on a different page? Has that ever happened to you?"

"Yes it has," I replied. "I used to think they were not listening to what I had been saying, but I think the explanation lies elsewhere. Here's an example. When my daughter was 14, she started attracting the attention of teenage boys. One night, at about a quarter to midnight, the phone rang, and it was one of those boys asking to speak to my daughter. Slipping into Outraged Parent mode, I demanded, *Do you know what time it is?!*

"Yeah," he said, *"It's about 11:45."*

Norman and I both laughed, and I added, "He had taken my question as a request for information rather than the rhetorical question is was intended to be, to underline the implicit rule of behaviour. I considered that rule of behaviour to be implicitly understood, but clearly it was not understood by that young man. Perhaps it was a difference in the rules of behaviour that apply in either his generation or his social group. I was quite amused, but it did make me realise that my social assumptions are not universally shared."

EMBEDDED ASSUMPTIONS

Norman then said, "I'm sure you know that assumptions of that kind are embedded in our daily conversations, and most of the time they are shared by those to whom you are speaking. But often we know which assumptions are shared, and we adjust our statements accordingly. Let me give you a couple of examples. If I said to you, *Petrol is getting more expensive,* I would be assuming that you knew the typical price of petrol today. But if you told me, *I won the Best Speaker award this evening* you'd be presuming that I knew about such awards at Toastmasters meetings. Even a simple question like *How's your slimming regime going?* assumes a prior knowledge of your attempt to lose weight. You couldn't ask a total stranger such a question. It would be meaningless.

"There is another side to the listening problem. It's about how information is presented to us. You see, most of us have a way of taking in new information and we struggle if it is offered in a different way. This is most common in communicating numbers. Radio broadcasters are often the worst offenders. In Ireland, for example, there is a radio programme on RTE1 radio that invites listeners to contact the station. In the course of the programme, the presenter would suddenly remember he had to give out the number and rattle off *51 double 5 1 is the number* or perhaps he said *515 double 1*. I could never be sure, partly because he spoke so quickly, but partly because the word 'double' got in the way. My personal preference would have been *five one five one one*. I emailed that suggestion to the radio station and they adopted it, although I'm not sure if I was responsible for the change.

"And while we are on the subject of implicit miscommunication, like your daughter's young man calling later than he should, let's also consider how we might deliberately mislead by implication. Suppose there had been an accident outside your house. The policemen asks you, *Did you witness the accident?* And you reply, *My window overlooks the scene.* Now, you may not have intended to mislead, but can you see how you haven't directly answered the question, but you have allowed the policemen to believe that you saw the incident.

"And then there is the classic response to a request for a reference on a former employee. You might say, *I cannot speak too highly of him.* It gets you out of the problem of not being allowed to give a poor reference, but the inference is there.

"Let's take a break, and then we'll say more about the language we use."

Chapter 14 Summary

Listening

The most underrated skill in verbal communication is listening. Yet there are few training courses in listening.

Peter Thomson recommends rapid repeating to focus the mind on the speaker and aid memory. There is, however, a difference between telling to inform and telling to educate. So always verify what your audience has taken in.

Remember Tracks 150 and 350, to explain why your listeners' attention will always drift, and loop back to help them catch up. Remember, too, that we all have embedded assumptions which make us hear what we expect rather than what was actually said.

That's why we sometimes have difficulty in understanding what was said. And why we can use language that tricks the listener into hearing what we did not say.

152

THE MAN WHO GAVE AWAY HIS LOTTERY WIN

Fifteen

Miscommunication

"Let's talk about miscommunication. What I mean by that is when the receiver hears or understands something that is different from the truth or reality. There are broadly two kinds – the accidental, which could arise out of ignorance, and the deliberate or intentional. The latter is rather complex, so let me first dispose of the accidental or unintended miscommunication. If my knowledge of a topic is either incorrect or incomplete, I could mislead you. That's quite straightforward, unless you disagree with what I tell you.

"Take a simple example. Suppose I stated that the moon is 2.4 million miles away. That could be a genuine mistake because I just did not know the right answer, or it could be a careless mistake, because I mis-remembered the numbers, which are 238,855 miles or 384,400 kilometres on average. Or it could even be that I wanted to test you.

153

"How would you react to that?

"If you have no idea how far away the moon is, you might just accept my false information and repeat it to others on some other occasion. Or you might suspect it sounds like a lot further than you thought it was, and decide to check it out later. Or you might even rub your chin and cast doubt on that figure of 2.4 million miles.

"The third option is the most contentious. It's when you know that what I said was incorrect. Should you put me right? If so, how would you do so? Of course, it depends on the context. If I happened to be your prospective father-in-law, or your boss at work, you might hesitate to correct me, because that might seem disrespectful, or because it might cause a row. And if the occasion happened in the presence of others, for example at a dinner party, it could spoil the whole evening.

WOULD YOU CORRECT HIM?

"Here's an actual example. A speaker I know, an established member of the Professional Speaking Association, wrote on Facebook that he wanted to construct *a pneumonic for his book that would soon be published.* Of course he knew that right word was mnemonic but, as he said, he wanted to see if anyone would notice. Or, as I remarked, if anyone would have the brass neck to suggest he did not know.

154

"So what's the answer? I got the answer from the example of a friend of mine who knows a bit about assertiveness. His advice was in two parts. First, he said, never feel you always have to correct someone else when they make a mistake, unless it is to halt the spread of a factoid. But secondly, develop a simple strategy for such situations. Have a form of words and a manner of delivery that is unlikely to give offence. In my example of the distance of the moon, you might smile and say, *Really? Is it that far? I think I read somewhere that it's only about 240,000 miles. Shall we look it up?*

"There are four important elements in that response. First, be as pleasant and un-confrontational as possible. Second, respond immediately, as in any conversation, where you are entitled to have an alternative opinion on any topic that arises. If you hesitate before casting doubt, you risk making me look and feel foolish. Third, attribute your version to a source elsewhere. That avoids a direct clash between my assertion and yours. And fourth, add the tag question, *Shall we look it up?* That implies we could both be wrong, so let's rely on a third party. Such a response avoids a clash and saves you from having to accept something you feel or know to be false.

"Now, that's about dealing with an unintentional piece of misinformation. What about deliberate misinformation? That's much more complex, and there are shades of grey. I remember a conversation between an atheist friend of mine and a Methodist minister. The atheist had a habit of challenging anyone's declared position, so he asked the minister, *Are you allowed to tell a lie?*

The minister had obviously been asked that question before and he was well prepared for it. He said, *There are 'situational ethics'. That's about doing what is right at the time. If the truth will do more harm, I will say what it takes to avoid the harm. That consideration will override any absolute moral standards.* He went on to explain that love and caring will outweigh other considerations. The primary guideline is this: 'who is to be helped' matters more than 'what is the law'.

WHAT IS A LIE?

"But let me return to the question of deliberate misinformation. Do you ever tell a lie?"

His question took me by surprise and I noticed that the context of our conversation influenced my reply. In a casual conversation with a friend I might shrug and admit to occasional "fibs", but it would always feel uncomfortable having to admit that I do not always tell the truth. And yet, I knew that we all bend the truth at times. Situational ethics are all very well, but that feels like a cop-out when directly confronted by the polygraph question. So I just nodded.

I remembered a film I had seen about a threat to the life of the US President. All his close staff and body guards had to take a lie detector test, in which a key question was, "Have you recently done anything that might endanger the life of the President?" One of his main bodyguards was having an affair with the First Lady, so he hesitated before answering No to the question. The polygraph noted the involuntary change in his heartbeat and registered it as a lie.

Norman let me off the hook when he said, "Good man. We all lie at times. Let's consider four main levels of deception in our speech. But even as we consider each in turn, let's not forget the encoding that takes place during conversations, the intention of the speaker and the process that goes on in the mind of the receiver or listener.

"First, there is the so-called white lie, when we bend the truth for social reasons. A form of situational ethics, if you like. A common example is when you lie to keep secret a surprise party. It serves the greater good to tell the lie. There are no adverse consequences and no one is offended by it. The key element here is the intention. In fact, the intention is exactly what defines the seriousness of the deception. Such lies are known as altruistic deception.

"The second level is when we suppress or exaggerate certain parts of the truth for a specific purpose. Speakers do this all the time. They take an incident in their own

157

lives and tailor it to the message they want to illustrate. They might leave out certain details and add in a few others to suit the narrative. I'm sure you'd agree that such a practice is perfectly acceptable, so long as it is not done for self-aggrandisement. Fishermen and golfers are renowned for exaggerating their exploits. It was th-a-a-a-a-t big! And some people say, *The older I get the better I was.* Most of the time that doesn't matter. It's just a bit of social lubrication.

DECEPTION BY IMPLICATION

"The third level of deliberate miscommunication is more serious. It is when you do not actually lie, but your reply leads me to an incorrect understanding of the facts. Politicians do this all the time. It's lying by implication or lying by omission, when some essential element is deliberately omitted from a report, for example. Here's an example. Question: What time did you get home last night? Answer: I was in bed by midnight. What was not stated was where that bed was.

"Another fertile area for this kind of deception is the advertising and marketing industry. For many years Reader's Digest based their direct marketing on a Prize Draw in which they would write to you, if you were on their list, implying either that you might already have won the £250,000 top prize in the Draw, or that your chances of winning would be improved by buying the product being offered. Careful copywriting avoided breaking the law, but created the excitement that induced people to buy the product. Research confirmed that people believed their chances in the Prize Draw were improved if they bought the product, although that was not so, nor was it ever claimed in the promotion.

"There may be more levels of deception, but let's call the fourth level the ultimate. It's the outright lie, a total fabrication intended to change or re-direct your thinking or behaviour. An example of this was when the Leave campaign in the UK's Brexit referendum promised to recover £350 million per week for the NHS. It was an outright lie, and the Leave campaigners led by Boris Johnson knew perfectly well that they were lying.

UNDERSTAND THE SWORDPLAY

"Now why have I detailed these four levels of deception? Because they are all strategies of communication. We need to understand the swordplay that each represents, and avoid being misled. Equally, we need to recognise when we ourselves conduct these manipulations of the truth. Conversations are intended to build trust as well as communicate information and exchange ideas.

"The language we use reflects the circumstances in which we live. And our language is changing. It is increasingly self-serving. Back in 1946 George Orwell said, *When the general atmosphere is bad, language must suffer.* Much more recently, Sherry Turkle, professor of social psychology at MIT, wrote a book called *Reclaiming Conversation: The Power of Talk in the Digital Age.* She said we must talk to one another more. She said that young people, in particular, allow themselves always to be distracted by their phones, creating increasingly shallow relationships. Emailing and texting is easier but less constructive. In conversation we discover and modify our own beliefs, we learn more about others, we build trust with them. But we need to understand what goes on.

"We need to develop the ability to evaluate what others tell us, in person and through the media. How can you tell when someone is lying? Sometimes their top lip will perspire. Other times the rate of hand gestures will change. That's because lying involves a greater share of the cognitive process, and that will change the pattern of unconscious movements. There are many signs of lying but don't become fixated on them. You are not a detective looking for the perpetrator of a crime.

"Notice inconsistencies and decide if you want to trust the person or not. Above all, take note of manipulations and avoid being guilty of them yourself."

Chapter 15 Summary

Miscommunication

There are several ways in which we mislead others, either accidentally or by design. We might make an incorrect claim or statement through our own ignorance or to test our listener, or deliberately use the wrong word to see what reaction we would get. Who would have the nerve to correct us?

One person said there is no obligation to correct anyone who makes a mistake, except to halt the spread of a factoid. But it is always useful to have developed a form of words that allows you to dispute a factual error without causing offence.

Politicians, among others, are practised in deception by implication or by omission. Why should we care about such things? Because language is suffering as we become more self-serving. And because we must talk to one another more, and avoid manipulations.

THE MAN WHO GAVE AWAY HIS LOTTERY WIN

Sixteen

The language we use

His mention of the word "manipulations" triggered a thought in my mind. I'm in the Persuasion business – sales, public speaking, training -- and "manipulation" is a charge frequently levelled at the sales process. Robert Cialdini, for example has written tens of thousands of words on the process of persuasion. I asked Norman what he thought of being persuasive in conversation, and how that fitted in with the objective of getting your point across in a meeting.

"Although that sounds like two different points," replied Norman, "I think they are both parts of the same principle. Let's take a big step back first, and then let's consider what happens in the minds of people who are faced with a choice in a sales situation.

"As I've said before, in most interactions between people there will be two positions: Supplicant and Dominant.

The Supplicant is the one with the need. The Dominant has the power. The roles will switch from time to time, according to the issue, and even between equals, one will be the Dominant. I am not saying that one person is seeking to dominate the other. It's just the natural position we assume in any transaction. In a sense we are conditioned to accept those positions. In our formative years, we are directed by our elders, by our teachers and by those in superior positions to ourselves.

SUPPLICANT OR DOMINANT

"As we grow older and discover our own aptitudes, we gain dominant positions from time to time, and we learn how to exercise the power of the one who has something that another person wants. We also learn what happens when someone overrides that process, when someone who should be supplicant but behaves dominantly. That's called bullying. When we recognize and accept our role, as either the Supplicant or the Dominant, it will determine not only our behaviour but also our language."

I said I got that, but wondered if there were a community or society that conditioned themselves differently, an egalitarian society in which no one sought to dominate. What would be the outcome of transactions in such a place.

Norman laughed and said, "There is such a place. It's called Sweden. The Swedes are famous for not making decisions. As one Swede has written, they hold meetings to find out if they are at that meeting to decide when to hold a meeting to talk about what happened at that meeting. Because everyone is equal, they seek consensus, so they all have to have their say, and then go and hear what their colleagues have to say, and so on, endlessly. They all listen and then they compromise. They aim for win-win in everything, and they avoid saying Yes or No. They prefer to say *maybe* or *it depends*. It drives foreigners mad, and the Swedes call such reactions hysterical.

"Essentially, the Swedes try to avoid conflict, so they may be the model to follow. They take time off, they have endless coffee breaks and leg-stretching breaks, but they work hard and are surprisingly effective. But the rest of the world operates more on the Supplicant-Dominant model for their transactions. And for the language they use.

"You raise a good point about manipulation and domination. So let me ask you to consider something that happens all the time in this country and other countries with a similar set of values. In a conversation both people start to speak at the same time. They both invite the other to go ahead first, and one of them does so. The other person has prevailed. Although it may seem that the person who proceeds to speak has won the point, actually it is the other person who made the decision about who should speak first.

COURTESY IS NOT PATRONISING

"Here's a similar situation, but it's one with overtones. A man and a woman approach a door together. With traditional courtesy, the man holds the door open for the woman. She goes through and then feels a slight resentment, as though she has been patronised. Not his intention, but she has been conditioned by today's battle for equality between the sexes. Reversing the coin, my grey hair has prompted women on trains and buses offering me their seat. I always accept, out of respect for their good intentions. However, I could easily allow myself to feel offended at the implication that I am elderly.

"Those who use persuasion professionally, sales people and therapists, for example, develop a style of speaking that embeds suggestions or even instructions in what seems to be ordinary conversation patterns. They prompt us to add the unspoken request or instruction and act upon it. This is known as the Milton Model and is frequently used in NLP and hypnosis.

"On the simplest level, there is a form of colloquial language that implies a request for action. If I said, *Could you stand up please?* Well, obviously you could, but you understand that I want you to actually do so. And there

166

is less resistance in you than if I said, *Stand up please.* Similarly, a hypnotist might say, *I wonder if you can recall a time when you felt totally relaxed?* Or, *I can see you looking relaxed and confident, smiling cheerfully, obviously looking forward to making that speech.*

"On one level you might say that these are simply polite ways of speaking, to make your requests more acceptable. But the more significant element is the way the listener's brain is engaged to receive, understand and act upon the embedded instruction. When you combine both, you get a model for more effective communication. That is to say, the speaker should A. adopt an attitude of respect and politeness, and B. use words like *could, would, should, might, may, will* and *can.* I know a man who always bows low when he shakes your hand and he habitually says, *Would you mind (doing something).* He's very popular.

"Those examples have a bearing on what we've been talking about today. And it's this:

"In this conversation I have aired some issues that will clarify how we communicate and connect with one another, and how that might affect our relationships. Why is that important? Because in even the best conversations only a small part is transferred and retained. The rest is either social lubrication or social adjustment.

167

SOCIAL ADJUSTMENT

"Here are some examples of social adjustment. Some may call them re-framing the relationship:

1. A man wrote on Facebook that he was re-starting running, having given it up 17 years ago when he had a double heart bypass. In reply someone wrote: *Since my triple last year I have done three 5Ks in one week.* What was his intention? It came across as an attempt to trump the original post.

2. James said he was being visited shortly by Megan, a well-known social media activist. A friend of his said, *Good. You'll be able to pick her brains on webinars.* He had re-framed the visit as a chance to benefit from a greater expert.

3. Peter is a writer. When he is writing he doesn't like to be disturbed. But his wife will call out and ask what he would like for dinner. If he answers her, he will break his concentration, and if he rebuffs her, he will upset her, so he ends up taking a break and keeping the peace. But it can result in a built-up resentment.

4. Farouk woke up one morning with a poem in his mind, so he wrote it down. It was a poem about unrequited love. His wife read it and said, *That poem is clearly not about me, so who is this other woman?* Farouk tried to explain that it was

just an idea that came to him, and he tore it up, but the harm was done.

5. Ben won a public speaking contest. A schoolmate told him, *I remember your elder brother was the debating champion at school.* The implication, however unintended, was to put him back to where he once was, inferior to his elder brother. That was his place, and nothing would change that.

REFRAMING CHANGES PERCEPTION

"There are countless such examples of put-downs and relationship reframing in everyday conversations and in high level meetings. Reframing changes the perception of what we say or do. So what is the answer? I think it requires a culture change. And that's where you come in, as a professional speaker. If you can influence your audiences to re-think the way they communicate and adopt a more sensitive attitude to one another, there could be less social discord, fewer confrontations, greater harmony.

"Today I have shared with you two vital principles on verbal communication, ideas on gaining acceptance, on being tolerant, about addressing the right audience, about porcupines making necessary adjustments, telling the right story, meeting expectations, listening skills and how we get it wrong. We've spoken about miscommunication and more, and you shared your Five

Questions that keep your sales people on track. I do hope you have found it both interesting and useful. Above all, I hope you now understand why I am keen to spread the word and get people making better use of the opportunities to exchange thoughts and ideas.

"Before I let you go, I want to return to the subject of Brexit. Now, I don't mean the final outcome, I mean the crossed wires and ill-will from the moment the unexpected result of the 2016 Referendum was announced. It was always about a change to the status quo. Those who voted Leave said they were unhappy about unrestricted immigration, about the raft of rules from Brussels, and about the money it was costing us to remain in the EU.

"What the Brexit campaign did was to give expression to the feeling that the British way of life, or more specifically the English way of life, had been eroded by the influx of foreigners. People blamed the EU, its silly rules, its bureaucracy, its citizens who spoke with unfamiliar accents and did not understand traditional English ways. If you examine what the Brexit campaigners said and what the Leave voters said after the referendum, I think you'll find they were not the same.

The hour was late and we had covered a lot of ground, but I felt there was much more we should be talking about. I wanted to explore further the idea that communication is both proactive and reactive – we

170

provoke and also react to our listeners, at the same time. I wanted to talk about the way we re-frame a conversation, sometime interrupting to correct a word or a point of grammar. When we do so we may not intend to spoil the narrative, but we reframe it, and that might carry a consequence for the relationship.

I wanted to discuss the effect of changing the emphasis within a phrase, to accentuate a different word, perhaps even the wrong word, and the effect that has on the message being received.

It was time to take my leave and consider returning another day to continue this fascinating discourse on the many ways we share our thoughts and ideas with each other. I thanked Norman for his hospitality and waved goodbye.

Chapter 16 Summary

The language we use

Persuasion in language recognises that there are two roles: Dominant and Supplicant. The Dominant has the power while the Supplicant has the need. The roles will determine the language we use.

The Milton Model is used in NLP and hypnosis, embedding instructions and commands in indirect suggestions, both to avoid resistance and to engage the listener's mind so that the necessary action takes place.

In many conversations there is social re-framing, in some to adjust the dominant-supplicant relationship, in others to enact a preferred agenda. But being sensitive to one another will reduce social discord and confrontations. How we manage that will affect our relationships.

THE MAN WHO GAVE AWAY HIS LOTTERY WIN

Seventeen

Closure

The next week was a busy one for me, so I made no effort to contact Norman Sinclair. However, he had given me much to think about, and throughout each day I was reminded of the many topics we had discussed. All the while I recalled how we had met – his unusual approach to the street sleepers, giving each of them a watch and a fifty pound note. At the same time he had hoped to meet someone like me, a professional speaker who could relay his ideas one-to-many. The two things were not connected, unless his charitable donations were designed to get someone like me to notice him and have yesterday's extended conversation.

In my notebook I had written, *The first truth about effective communication – it's not about Transmission, but Reception. About how it is received and understood.* It came back to me strongly when I was making a phone call to my electricity supplier. I spoke to a woman in customer service to ask why my bill was higher than the national average and she became defensive. She said they had

173

checked my meter and found it working satisfactorily, she said she didn't know what machines I was running. She said there was nothing wrong with the bill. And then she asked if I wanted to make a complaint.

I hadn't rung to make a complaint. Rather, I was looking for information, for guidance on ways to reduce my bill. But she heard my query as a complaint. The incident reminded me of what Norman had said about the first truth – that what matters is how the message is received and understood. I thought about that for a while, and then I recalled something else that Norman had said, that dialogues can be about domination, about who has the upper hand.

CUSTOMER SERVICE?

The customer service person had manoeuvred me into a position where I would be the loser, whatever I said. If I said I wanted to make an official complaint, I would have to provide evidence of fault in the meter, the supply mechanism, or the invoicing: evidence that I would find hard or impossible to find, even if wanted to. And if I said I did not want to make a complaint, I would be on the back foot, having to justify making the call in the first place. It would have been hard to answer if she had then asked me, *Are you satisfied with the service we provide?*

If I questioned her attitude, we would have had a row, a battle I did not want. Yet that same attitude had made it difficult to respond favourably. So I just took a deep breath and said, *No, I was just looking for some information. Where will I find some guidance on keeping my bills down?* Predictably, she was unable to help me. Her filters were in place to treat all such calls as complaints and clearly she just wanted to be able to tick the box, Complaint Resolved.

The incident stayed with me for most of the day, and made me aware of the games people play, and the hidden, unspoken messages that cause so much trouble. The language of thought. Plus the woman's fragile ego.

Yesterday's conversation had given me new ways to make sense of a common miscommunication. She hadn't understood what I wanted. Either she had a training need or simply lacked the ability to understand the question behind my question. After all, don't we often sense that what a person is saying is not what they mean? And don't we then say something like, *I think you are really saying / asking this?*

For my part, I should have been more specific, telling her from the start that I was looking for some guidance on keeping my bills down. A classic miscommunication, yet one of which the customer service woman was blithely unaware.

THE 3 TRUTHS OF COMMUNICATION

It reminded me of the **First Truth** of communication, that it is not about transmission but rather about how it is received and understood.

And that led me on to the **Second Truth**, which is not to speak to be understood, but rather to avoid being misunderstood. I remembered the vivid examples of the Charge of the Light Brigade, the Massacre at Wounded Knee and the Scandinavian whose cross-cultural misconnect caused his Indian counterpart to lose face.

Most especially I remembered the **Third Truth**, which is about the way we make our listeners feel. Quite unnecessarily, the customer service woman had made me feel uncomfortable and then angry. Echoes of Mrs May's intransigence in the House of Commons, when she refused to alter any of her red lines on Brexit!

I had a business presentation to prepare, and for that it was helpful to remind myself of the Five Questions I prompt sales people to answer before making a pitch:

1. **Why?** My purpose
2. **Why not?** Believing I can satisfy the customer's needs
3. **What?** My Added Value
4. **So what?** The consequence of my proposition
5. **What next?** Leaving the door open

I remembered also the detailed image of an 18th century courtier with an important message for the king, and that guided the tone of my presentation as well as my preparation, structure, the language I would use and the emotional connection in my script.

At some point during the day my wife asked me about my conversation with Customer Services at the electricity company. She was aghast at what I told her and wanted to know if I would make a complaint. I said I would not, and nor would I let it bother me for the very good reason that I could not change anything about it, and was not going to allow the incident to colour my approach to the business presentation.

In my presentation I intended to deliver some unexpected facts, backed by statistical evidence, but I remembered the conversation we had had about the power of stories. My mind went back to a meeting I had attended at Toastmasters years before, when the late Philip Smee gave us a lasting insight into the myth of the Mehrabian statistics, the discredited claim that words contribute only 7% of the meaning. Norman had mentioned that during our marathon conversation. And I decided to tell that story when delivering the figures I was going to use, bringing Philip and the incident's lasting impact to life.

When I had completed my first draft I looked through it with a critical eye, asking myself what was different or unexpected about it, and whether it identified and sought to satisfy the expectations or needs of my proposed audience. Playing devil's advocate I challenged every claim, every assumption, anything which was capable of being misconstrued. I even changed every "male" reference to a gender-neutral one. No point in risking giving offence to even one person.

It had been a constructive day, preparing the presentation in the light of my previous day's intensive dialogue with Normal Sinclair, reminding myself of the main points about verbal communication and implementing as many as possible. I resolved to take the presentation down to see Norman one day soon.

A FRESH MYSTERY

The following week I rang Norman's number but got no reply. As I had reason to go to Croydon anyway, I thought I'd just nip over to Crockham and knock on his door. When my business in Croydon was over, I did just that.

There was no sign of life at the house, and the garage door was shut. Even more baffling was the estate agent's For Sale board, which I had not noticed on my previous visit. I rang the number on the board.

"Are you interested in buying the property?" asked the man who answered.

"No, I'm not," I replied. "I'm just trying to contact Normal Sinclair."

"Are you a relation or a friend?" the fellow wanted to know.

"More of a business acquaintance," I said, not wanting to go into details. "Why do you ask?"

There was a brief pause, as though he was making his mind up about something, then, "Well, you see, Mr Sinclair has just died. Could you tell me your name, please?"

When I told him who I was he said, "Hold on," he said, "just a minute." And I could hear him opening a drawer and rustling through some papers. "Yes, here it is," he said, picking up the phone again. "I have an envelope here with your name on it. My Sinclair left it when he gave us instructions to sell the house. Said to pass it on to you. That's why I asked your name. I was expecting you to get in touch soon."

A VERY SPECIAL MESSAGE

Even more surprising was the handwritten note inside the envelope I collected from the estate agent. The note read:

Thanks for the most interesting time we spent together. I had hoped to meet someone like you. I was encouraged to learn that you shared my views on the process of communication, and that you might be able to share them with a wider audience. I told you I had set up a Trust that is putting together programmes in communication skills. I have given them your phone number and they will contact you to find out if you want to be involved. One more thing: we need to re-discover the virtue of enjoying our own company, through Solitude:

> *Trying to communicate,*
> *It seems we've lost our way.*
> *We peer at screens and text our thoughts;*
> *What drives us on, this most of all,*
> *To seek connection that affirms*
> *That we are not alone. And anyone will do.*
> *The solitude of singleness can surely gain us more,*
> *A private place inhabited by only you or me,*
> *At peace, content, when on our own,*
> *Hearing what we think, knowing what we know,*
> *Happy with the way we are,*
> *Alone but never lonely, and enjoying*
> *Solitude.*

Warmly,
Norman.

Attached was a printed slip that said, "Here's a simple scenario to help you remember most of our conversation. Imagine checking into a hotel. Here are the main steps and what they signify:

Steps in the scenario	What they signify
1. First impressions	How do you come across to your listeners?
2. Doorway. How easy is it to enter? Remember it is also the exit	Ease of entry into your topic and Outcome you want to achieve
3. You walk up to Reception and state your name. The Receptionist mishears what you said and cannot find your booking	Remember the Three Truths of Communication: Reception, Avoid Misunderstanding & How you make them feel
4. You get your key with a tag attached to make it easy for the key to be returned to the hotel if lost	Tag questions make it easier to accept what you say
5. The Receptionist calls a porter to help with your luggage, repeating your name	This is Respect
6. She has a friendly, pleasant way of speaking	Tone of voice
7. You are directed to the correct lift	Right audience
8. On the wall of the lift is a poster for a production of Snow White	Story
9. Arriving on your floor you cannot see the signs for your room and head in the wrong direction	Miscommunication
10. You ask for help from a maid with little English	Tolerance

11. The door to your room is stiff so you call Reception. They send a man with fresh towels	Not listening
12. You put it right and they send someone else with an oil can	Social Lubrication/Reframing
13. As he leaves the door slams hard	Making an impact
14. As you unpack, you check the bathroom, the iron, hair dryer, tea maker and hangers.	Expectations
15. On the desk you find the Feedback form	Lasting impressions

In a separate box there were a couple of dozen watches and a corresponding bunch of £50 notes, with a note saying, "Please keep up the good work!"

Chapter 17 Summary

Closure

Spent the next week catching up on admin. Had a trying phone call with someone in Customer Services at my electricity supplier. My quest for advice was translated into a complaint, just to enable a box to be ticked.

Reminded myself of the Three Truths of Communication and my own Five Questions when outlining my business presentation.

Dropping in on Norman the next week, I learned that he died. But he had left me some notes to make it easy to remember what we talked about, and his wish that I would continue his good work.

184

About the author

Phillip Khan-Panni is a Founder Director and Honorary Fellow of the Professional Speaking Association, UK and Ireland. He is the author of six books on communication skills, co-author of two more, plus one of poetry and one partial memoir.

Following a career in sales, advertising and direct marketing, in 1994 he started a training business, PKP Communicators, specialising in verbal communication, and co-founded 4C International Ltd. (cross-cultural communication) in 2000. He has spoken and run training programmes in 20 countries.

His speciality is persuasive communication, developed initially in a selling career which included 13 awards in his first year, setting the company record of 89% conversion when selling Management Consultancy, and tripling Classified Advertising revenue at the Daily & Sunday Express in less than one year.

In public speaking he has won numerous awards, including Inaugural UK Business Speaker of the Year,

Toastmasters International's Anglo-Irish champion three times, TMI Inter-District Champion, and is the UK's first ever second place winner in the World Championship of Public Speaking.

His first wife died tragically in 1991 and he now lives in Ireland with his second wife, Evelyn, a retired psychiatric nurse tutor and Distinguished Toastmaster. This is his 11th published book, but his first full-length work of fiction.

His websites are:
http://phillipkhan-panni.com
http://SpeakingAndPresentationSkills.com
http://CVsThatWork.com

Printed in Poland
by Amazon Fulfillment
Poland Sp. z o.o., Wrocław